Prides

The Lions of Moremi

Prides

The Lions *of* Moremi

Text by

PIETER KAT

Photography by

CHRIS HARVEY

Smithsonian Institution Press
Washington, D.C.

Published in the United States of America
by the Smithsonian Institution Press
in association with Southern Book Publishers (Pty) Ltd
(a member of the New Holland Struik Publishing Group)
P.O. Box 5563
Rivonia 2128
Republic of South Africa

Library of Congress Cataloging-in-Publication Data
Harvey, Chris, 1947-
    Prides : the lions of Moremi / Chris Harvey & Pieter Kat.
        p.   cm.
    Includes bibliographical references.
    ISBN 1-56098-838-X (alk. paper)
    1. Lions–Botswana–Moremi Wildlife Reserve. I. Kat, Pieter W.
II. Title.
    QL737.C23H375   2000
    599.757'096883–dc21   99-38644

Map by **Chris Harvey**
Cover design by **Lyndall du Toit**
Designed and typeset by **Lyndall du Toit**
Set in Garamond
Reproduction by **Hirt & Carter Repro**
Printed and bound by **Craft Print**
    (Pte) Ltd
Manufactured in Singapore,
not at government expense
07 06 05 04 03 02 01 00   5 4 3 2 1

Dedication

To my daughters Philippa,
Frieda and Marieke.

Pieter Kat

To Maggi and Niki.

Chris Harvey

Preface

The title of this book, *Prides: The Lions of Moremi*, conveys a traditional message about lions. For the past four years, we have been privileged to observe these complex and highly intelligent animals in one of the last remaining wild places on earth. Many entrenched assumptions about lions have been at variance with our observations, and we suggest several conventional notions about prides should be abandoned. We should probably think of lion prides as associations of individuals joined by bonds of familiarity, shared experience, and mutual benefit rather than a tightly knit group of genetically related females. Pride males are not always the fathers of the cubs, and cubs in a pride might not be closely related. Lions are flexible opportunists who maintain a loose sociality that benefits their reproductive success, but simultaneously challenges their ill-suited reproductive system. In this book, we propose that a revision of our traditional perceptions would greatly benefit conservation of these magnificent carnivores.

Contents

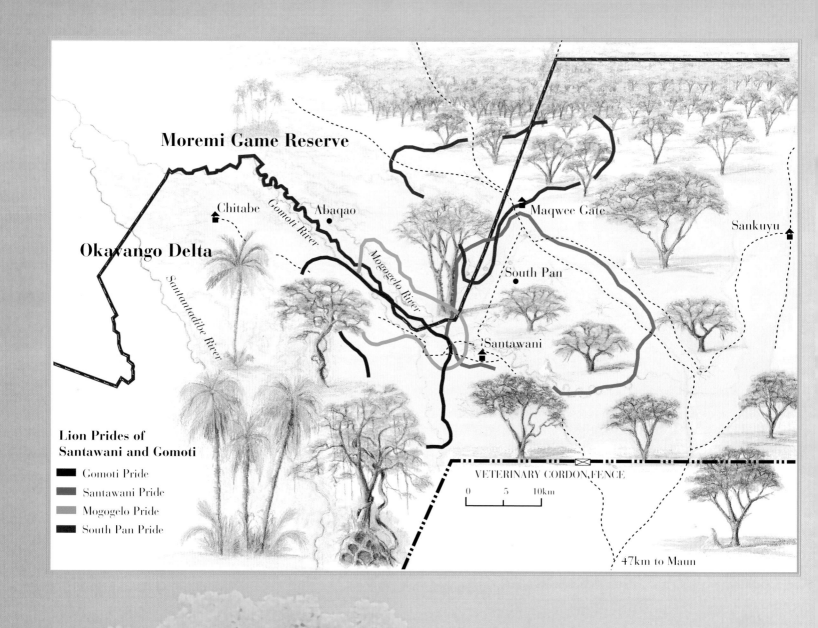

Moremi Game Reserve

Okavango Delta

Chitabe

Abaqao

Gomoti River

Santantadibe River

Mogogelo River

Maqwee Gate

Sankuyu

South Pan

Santawani

**Lion Prides of
Santawani and Gomoti**

- Gomoti Pride
- Santawani Pride
- Mogogelo Pride
- South Pan Pride

VETERINARY CORDON FENCE

0   5   10km

47km to Maun

The Prides

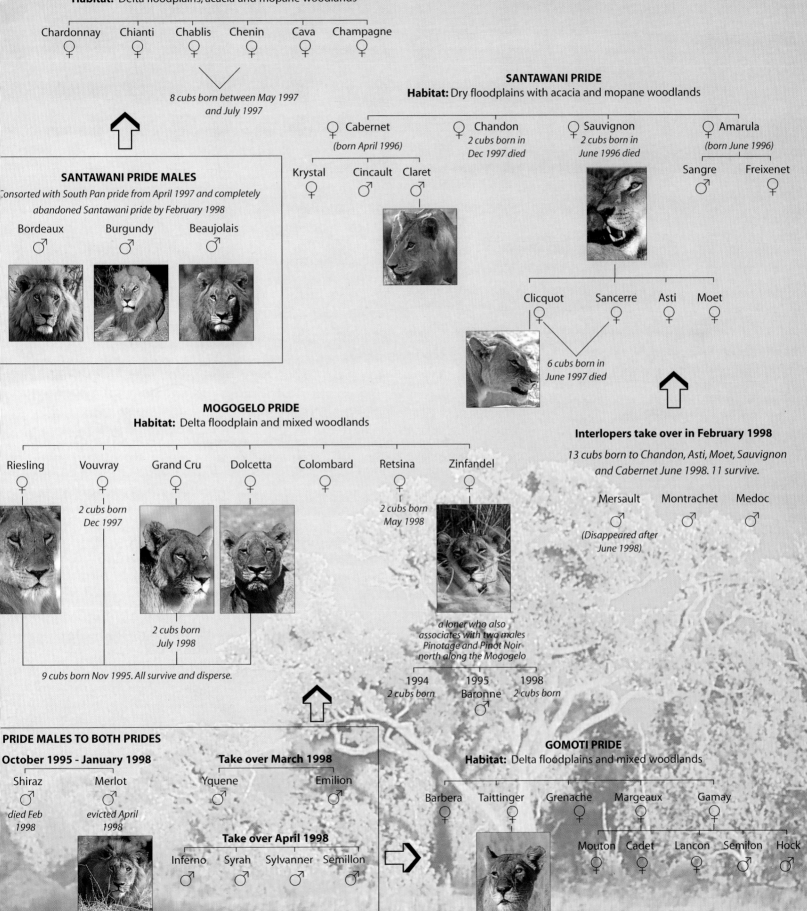

SOUTH PAN PRIDE FEMALES
Habitat: Delta floodplains, acacia and mopane woodlands

| Chardonnay ♀ | Chianti ♀ | Chablis ♀ | Chenin ♀ | Cava ♀ | Champagne ♀ |

8 cubs born between May 1997 and July 1997

SANTAWANI PRIDE
Habitat: Dry floodplains with acacia and mopane woodlands

♀ Cabernet *(born April 1996)* — Krystal ♀, Cincault ♂, Claret ♂

♀ Chandon *2 cubs born in Dec 1997 died*

♀ Sauvignon *2 cubs born in June 1996 died*

♀ Amarula *(born June 1996)* — Sangre ♂, Freixenet ♀

Clicquot ♀ — Sancerre ♀ — Asti ♀ — Moet ♀

6 cubs born in June 1997 died

SANTAWANI PRIDE MALES
Consorted with South Pan pride from April 1997 and completely abandoned Santawani pride by February 1998

| Bordeaux ♂ | Burgundy ♂ | Beaujolais ♂ |

Interlopers take over in February 1998

13 cubs born to Chandon, Asti, Moet, Sauvignon and Cabernet June 1998. 11 survive.

Mersault ♂   Montrachet ♂   Medoc ♂

(Disappeared after June 1998)

MOGOGELO PRIDE
Habitat: Delta floodplain and mixed woodlands

| Riesling ♀ | Vouvray ♀ | Grand Cru ♀ | Dolcetta ♀ | Colombard ♀ | Retsina ♀ | Zinfandel ♀ |

Vouvray: *2 cubs born Dec 1997*

Grand Cru: *2 cubs born July 1998*

Retsina: *2 cubs born May 1998*

Zinfandel: *a loner who also associates with two males Pinotage and Pinot Noir north along the Mogogelo*

9 cubs born Nov 1995. All survive and disperse.

1994 *2 cubs born*   1995 Baronne ♂   1998 *2 cubs born*

PRIDE MALES TO BOTH PRIDES

October 1995 - January 1998

| Shiraz ♂ | Merlot ♂ |

Shiraz: *died Feb 1998*

Merlot: *evicted April 1998*

Take over March 1998

| Yquene ♂ | Emilion ♂ |

Take over April 1998

| Inferno ♂ | Syrah ♂ | Sylvanner ♂ | Semillon ♂ |

GOMOTI PRIDE
Habitat: Delta floodplains and mixed woodlands

| Barbera ♀ | Taittinger ♀ | Grenache ♀ | Margeaux ♀ | Gamay ♀ |

Mouton ♀   Cadet ♀   Lancon ♂   Semilon ♂   Hock ♂

Introduction

Among the world's predators, there is arguably none that quickens our passion more than the lion. Richly represented in mythology, art, and parable, lions play a major role in the heritage of a diversity of cultures. What are the roots of this attraction to lions? Their sleek beauty and latent power, their grace and serene elegance must play a part, but it is also likely that our fascination stems from an ancestral respect and fear. At one time in our not too distant past we closely shared our environment with these supreme predators. As social carnivores, we shared their lifestyle and competed for food and territory.

Anthropologists believe that early hominids scavenged carcasses from predators, and that the development of the first weapons was a direct result of having to share the savannas with dangerous carnivores. In this sense, we owe lions a debt of gratitude – more than any other animal, they forced our ancestors to sharpen their wits and senses. In Africa, where many people still live with lions, no animal evokes greater awe, fear, and respect. Among tribes like the Maasai, killing a male lion with a spear is the ultimate test of manhood and bravery, and the lion's skin is worn as a testimonial to this act of paramount courage.

Since we began our project four years ago, we have become equally captivated by lions, and have formed a strong commitment to their study and informed conservation. We live in the study area all year, and the camp consists of five big bedroom tents, a kitchen/dining area covered with a large fly sheet, and a large mess tent that serves as a living room, library, and office. The study area encompasses the southeastern section of the Moremi Game Reserve and two adjoining community-based natural resource management areas.

The need for the research grew out of initial discussions with the Botswana Department of Wildlife and National Parks, where a study of lions had received high priority because of their economic and conservation importance. We began our

Opposite Lions of the Mogogelo pride use the elevation of a termite mound to watch for prey.

Above A lion contemplates crossing one of the many waterways of the Okavango Delta.

Above *After July, when drainages like the Mogogelo have been filled by the seasonal Okavango flood, the lions frequently ambush thirsty animals at the water's edge.*

work in October 1995, sharing a camp with John McNutt, an African wild dog researcher who had worked in the area since 1989. In April 1996, we were able to move to the disused Santawani lodge, and we recently made a third move to this camp near the Gomoti River.

We live simply but pleasantly – as a good friend of ours rightly points out, any fool can be uncomfortable in the bush! The town of Maun is a two hour drive from the study site, and because it is the centre of Botswana's tourist industry, provides us with all our basic necessities as well as some unexpected luxuries. Maun is where we receive our mail, faxes, and e-mails, socialise, repair our vehicles, and attend to bureaucracy. Town days are usually a flurry of activity – snatched conversations, communications, purchases, and perhaps a meal or two – before we return to our tented camp and the peace of the bush and the lions.

Good field research requires good support facilities, and our needs include such esoteric items as dry ice, liquid nitrogen, absolute ethanol, voltage regulators and inverters, radiocollars, biopsy darts, and cryotubes. Suppliers in South Africa, Great Britain, and the United States meet all our needs, and Maun is a tribute to the uniqueness of Botswana – where else in the world is a real wilderness separated from a major supply centre by little more than 40 kilometres?

We are concerned about the conservation status of lion populations, especially those in west and central Africa. Lions have probably been on the decline for centuries, and the introduction of livestock to the African savannas and the growth of human populations not surprisingly spelled disaster. As large, dangerous predators, they had to make way wherever friction occurred. Remember that this species once occurred in Europe, the

Left November, and the water in the Mogogelo marsh is turning to mud. The exposed hippos are forced to crowd together in dwindling pools and become aggressive and irritable.

Below Stressed and weakened, the hippos become prospective prey for opportunistic lions.

Middle East, India, and most of Africa. Today, one remnant population remains in India, the North African Barbary lion is a distant memory, and viable African lion populations only exist in a few scattered reserves south of the Sahara. Where do the large populations of lions occur in Africa? Probably northern Botswana, the Kruger National Park in South Africa, and the Serengeti National Park in Tanzania can be considered strongholds with more than 2 000 lions each. Good estimates exist for Etosha National Park in Namibia, Queen Elizabeth National Park in Uganda, Hwange National Park in Zimbabwe, the Masai Mara Reserve in Kenya and the Selous Reserve in Tanzania, but here lions are counted by hundreds or less. But what about the rest of Africa? The simple answer is that for most other countries, we just do not know how many lions remain. We remain confident that lions remain in Chad, the Central African Republic,

Cameroon, and perhaps Mali and Niger, but what are the long-term prospects for these populations? Are there any management plans to conserve these lions? We suspect from trends observed among other wildlife species that the western African lions might represent some unique genotypes, which makes them even more important for conservation of biodiversity.

We hope that we will be pleasantly surprised when information is gathered, but in the meantime are saddened by the complacency about the status of this majestic species. Even the remaining large populations are at risk: canine distemper killed many hundreds of lions in the Serengeti, tuberculosis has been detected among the Kruger Park lions, and dozens of lions are shot each year in Botswana to protect livestock.

However we are concerned that a more insidious problem may have a very negative impact upon lions: quite simply, we do not know enough about their basic biology.

Lion research – the status quo

Given our historic captivation with lions, it is surprising that so many aspects of their basic biology have remained poorly understood. This is not for a want of research: lions have been studied in Tanzania, Kenya, Uganda, South Africa, Namibia, Botswana, Zimbabwe, Zambia, and India. From these studies, a number of 'facts' about

Above As the rain subsides, Shiraz rises and shakes his sodden mane in almost defiant gesture at being so humbled. The dry season that had just passed was to be his last.

Left The first weeks of November are a time of anticipation, but this rainbow is not a good omen for the marsh lions, for their season of plenty is over. The game will disperse back to the woodlands and into the territories of other lions.

lions have now become well publicised. Any safari guidebook will inform the reader that lions are the only social cat species; that they live in prides composed of males, females, and their cubs; and that their society is matrilineal. Adult females in a pride form strong and lifelong bonds reinforced by the birth of cubs. Females raise cubs communally, and suckle each other's young. Members of different prides never mix. Young males are evicted from their natal prides and lead a nomadic existence until they attain the necessary size and strength to take over a pride of their own. When this happens, the new males immediately impose a stern rule that involves infanticide of cubs and expulsion of subadults. Females in a pride are always related, but males can form coalitions composed of non-related individuals.

The list goes on, and includes information about how and when lions hunt, what prey they take, why lions roar, how many times a lioness has to be mated before she conceives, etc. The overall picture that emerges is a rather cosy and neat one: lions live in secure prides and the behaviour of individuals can be predicted on the basis of their strong social and familial bonds. Pride males mate with pride females, the paternity of cubs is clear, and males and females protect their reproductive investment. This neat package satisfies us, the human observers, because it reinforces our concepts of the orderliness of nature and our ability to deduce patterns from complex systems. We are content, but meanwhile,a considerable mythology has become established.

Much of the scientific information on lions gathered to date comes from a long-term study conducted in the Serengeti. The study was initiated by one of the most eminent field biologists of our time, Dr. George Schaller. He began the study in 1966, and, in the space of three years, collected an amazing amount of information on a number of prides around the Serengeti Research Institute. George Schaller was the first to seriously study lions, and his contributions are significant despite the lack of reliable radiotelemetry. His dedication was awe-inspiring. The study was continued and enlarged by several people, perhaps most notably Drs. Craig Packer and Ann Pusey, who are still active in the project today. When we began this study in the Okavango in 1995, we were principally interested in determining what diseases were circulating among lions in northern Botswana. After all, if lions had been monitored for more than thirty years, all the basic information concerning lions had surely been collected, and lions must be among the best-studied animals in the world! But the more we became involved in our study, the more we realised that either the Okavango lions were different from all other lions previously studied, or, more likely, that many aspects of lion life were inadequately understood. Clearly, better and more scientifically robust explanations were needed for the way lions were behaving.

The study of wild animals requires close observation in their natural surroundings. Field biology is one of the most dynamic biological disciplines, and has its roots in the early expeditions of Charles Darwin and Alfred Russell Wallace. Their unclut-

tered observations of populations in the wild led to some of the most significant discoveries in biological science. In more recent years, field biology has become dominated by behavioural biologists, and this has perhaps resulted in the notebook-and-binoculars image that is evoked when the discipline is mentioned. However, good field biologists these days need a diverse biological training that includes familiarity with population genetics, evolution, ecology, behaviour, reproductive physiology, and animal health. We simply do not have the luxury to indulge in esoteric or narrowly focused research projects: such is the pressure on natural populations of wild animals that we are largely forced to conserve a few scattered assemblages. All conservation issues are urgent, and the best way to gather the

Opposite above *The lions' afternoon rest is disturbed by strong winds that herald the arrival of the first heavy downpour.*

Opposite below *A bolt of lightning and a deafening crash of thunder alarm the lions.*

Below *Temperatures drop quickly as the rain drenches the great Shiraz, who patiently endures the discomfort.*

volume of necessary information is by designing projects to be as broad-based as possible. Genetics, reproduction, and disease are as important in conservation and management plans as ecology and behaviour, but there are few studies that truly integrate these disciplines.

In this book, we will introduce many new ideas about lions. Since these ideas will be based on evolutionary, ecological, and reproductive principles, the underlying concepts might at first seem difficult to grasp. We will not attempt to gloss over these concepts, and will instead provide explanations of the theories and processes to make their understanding easier. Books on lions can be very dry or very fluffy: the latter more about the trials and tribulations of the authors as they struggle to survive rainstorms, heat waves, recalcitrant vehicles, bouts of malaria, and marauding hyenas. The former often use language unintelligible to the layman, and the reader becomes disinclined to wade through pages of graphs and tables. This book is meant to provide an alternative. We hope that by describing our journey, we will encourage contemplation rather than presumption.

Let us give you an example. It is often stated that lions are unique among cats in that they are social. This is such a well-known 'fact' that it has rarely been questioned. However, members of the lion genus *Panthera* most likely evolved from solitary ancestors. Certainly, all living *Panthera* species like tigers, jaguars, and especially leopards are solitary. Females of those species obviously form associations with their cubs, but males generally affiliate with females only to reproduce. Sociality among lions therefore likely represents a relatively 'new' adaptation. Not surprisingly, lions differ from other social animals in a number of important aspects: there is no dominance structure in the pride; females form fusion-fission groups in which membership can change daily; and it is only on very rare occasions that all males and females in the pride are together. Another significant observation is that female lions are reproductively like solitary cats. Lions are induced ovulators, which means that while a lioness may come into oestrus, she will not usually ovulate until she is mated. This makes perfect sense as an adaptation for a solitary animal: there is no guarantee that males will be in the neighbourhood when a female comes into oestrus. If there is no ovulation, a female will only have to wait a comparatively short time before her next oestrus. For lions this

form of reproduction makes much less sense, and seems to represent an inherited feature passed along from their solitary ancestors. Lions are without a doubt the most social of cats, but it is important to remember that their sociality is encumbered by a solitary inheritance.

Prides are probably best thought of as a group of adult female lions who associate with each other to reproduce, raise cubs, and hunt. Group membership is fluid, and can change radically as cubs become independent, or when new males take over a pride. Pride members often seem eager to assert their individuality, and the entire pride is very rarely seen together. Without dependent cubs, female groups can change composition daily, and females are frequently encountered alone. Prides, as we will see in a later chapter, can be rather loosely structured entities, and we strongly believe that members are held together by bonds of familiarity rather than familiality.

One of the most important lessons we have learned is that animals of this level of complexity and intelligence will require a long-term research commitment. How intelligent are lions? A very telling example was shown by Vouvray, one of the Mogogelo pride females. Deception is seen as one of the most complex of all animal behaviours because it requires abstract thinking. The deceiver needs to

Left *The Okavango takes six months to wind its way to this edge of the Delta.*

Below *Most of Africa is not composed of endless savanna, but is rather a mosaic of savanna, trees and shrubs.*

carefully evaluate the situation, think ahead, and then execute a plan that considers a predicted reaction. Consequently, there are few examples of truly deceptive behaviour, even among primates. Vouvray, however, recently showed us that she was capable of just that. She had discovered an impala killed by a cheetah, which she appropriated and dragged into some thick bush. After she ate some of the carcass, she headed back to the rest of the pride resting about half a kilometre away. As she approached, she called the cubs, intending to let them finish off the remains.

Unfortunately, the two pride males also responded to her calls. She was now faced with a dilemma: how could she prevent the males from eating and yet let the cubs get their fill? At first she lay down about 200 metres from the hidden impala and feigned a total lack of interest. This did not achieve much, as the males lay down next to her. Then she made another plan: she led the cubs over a kilome-

Below The grasses growing in the more fertile soils around the woodlands are highly nutritious and the herbivores have markedly improved in condition by the time their foals and calves arrive early in the wet season.

tre in the opposite direction to have a drink at the river. The males still followed her, but as they were drinking she called the cubs again and trotted back to the carcass. Unfortunately, the cubs had now become confused and did not respond fast enough. The males caught up with them as they reached the carcass, and foiled the plan. Nevertheless, Vouvray executed a complex plan, and had come close to deceiving the males.

The Okavango Delta

It is not surprising that most of the initial research on wild carnivores was done in the Serengeti and other places with similar habitats. Wide-open, short grass plains allow for optimal observation, and much of what we know about African wild dogs, hyenas, cheetahs, and lions is derived from those studies. But most of Africa is not composed of endless savanna: rather, much of Africa is a mosaic of savannas, trees and shrubs. This diversity of habitats is probably most richly represented in the Okavango Delta region of Botswana.

The Okavango River originates as small streams in the highlands of Angola, and the river then flows south and east until it encounters the endless thirst of the Kalahari Desert. The Kalahari was probably one of the world's first deserts, and it was formed many millions of years ago in the centre of the Gondwanan supercontinent. The Kalahari sands stretch from the Congo Basin deep into South Africa. Plate movements have since broken up that southern supercontinent and moved land masses like Africa, India, and South America further apart. The Kalahari has remained in the centre of southern Africa, and is crossed with active fault lines. As the Okavango River leaves the Caprivi region of Namibia and enters Botswana, the waters slow, the river begins to meander, and finally splits into the many tributaries that form the Delta. In fact, the total difference in elevation from one end of the delta to the other is only 62 metres over 250 kilometres. Near Maun, eastward flow of the river is blocked by the Thamalakane fault, and slight shifts along other fault lines regularly change the pattern of the water's flow. Over the last few years, for example, the bulk of the water has flowed along the western part of the Delta, and areas that were dry for a decade have been extensively flooded. Seen from the air, the Delta was clearly more extensive even 20 years ago, and is a shadow of its former self when Livingstone described the area. Nevertheless, it is still the largest inland delta in Africa, a unique oasis in the middle of the dry Kalahari.

A wide diversity of habitats is present in the Delta ecosystem, including permanent swamps, seasonal rivercourses and dry floodplains, acacia forests and mopane woodlands. Transitions among these habitats can take place over a few kilometres, and this is what makes the region so fascinating for a study of carnivores. A single lion pride territory can include five distinct habitat types, and neigh-

Above left *Browsers and mixed feeders like eland can extract moisture from their food during the dry season in the woodland of Santawani.*

Above centre *Giraffe are particularly vulnerable when drinking; but unlike the forest lions of Santawani, the lions of the Mogogelo marsh show little interest in them.*

Above right *Elephants add to the dust in the air with their frequent dust-baths.*

Left *In the woodlands surrounding the Delta, pans fill with water and herds arrive in hundreds. These migrations rearrange the distribution of prey in the region and the wet season is a time of considerable activity for the lions.*

bouring prides can inhabit areas radically different in the availability of water and prey.

The Okavango is a place of varied seasons. The worst of the heat comes in October. Daytime temperatures soar into the mid-forties, and a relentless sun burns the remaining stalks of grass to the consistency of parchment. Rain has not fallen since March, and even the largest rain water pans have turned to dust by August. Water-dependent species like zebra, elephant, and buffalo have long since sought refuge in the permanent swamps, and only giraffe, kudu, and impala remain in the drier areas. The lions suffer as much from the heat as we do, and move as little as possible during the day. Strangely, this is a time of plenty for predators. Even formidable animals like giraffe and elephant, weakened as they are by poor nutrition and the long treks they make to find water, fall prey to the lions. Those prides with territories that include a source of water have the easiest time of all: the lions need only wait in a shady spot close to a river or pool and wait for their meals to be delivered.

The first weeks of November are a time of anticipation. Clouds begin to build during the day, and often there is the sound of distant thunder. The barren and dry floodplains seem to come alive overnight as tsessebe and the first zebra move out of the Delta with the prospect of rain. The first showers arrive tenuously, with just enough rain to dimple the scorched earth. There is a sense of expectation in the air, and the disappointment as the clouds dissipate in the evening is tangible. Then one day the thunder is closer, and the smell of rain arrives like a provocative perfume. The effect of the arrival of the rains is both dramatic and swift. Almost immediately grass seeds germinate, and a bright green carpet erupts from the sand. Pans and depressions fill with water, and elephant, buffalo, zebra, and wildebeest arrive in their hundreds. Ducks and geese appear, thousands of white storks arrive on their migration from the north, and the nights resonate with the chorus of toads and frogs.

During the wet season, herbivores embark on a migration that takes them away from the Delta and into the acacia and mopane woodlands. The nutritional quality of various grasses differs considerably, and during the last months of the dry season, herbivores have to make do with low-quality fodder often deficient in necessary nutrients and minerals. Grasses growing in the more fertile soils of the floodplains and forests are highly nutritious, and

Right Although lions are the most social cats, it is important to remember their solitary inheritance.

the herbivores need this boost to improve their condition and to provide milk for their new-born calves and foals. The migration re-arranges the distribution of prey in the region, and the wet season for the lions is a time of considerable activity. Especially those lions with territories that include permanent water find themselves having to wander far afield in search of prey. As a consequence, they often trespass into the territories of neighbouring prides, trying to snatch a quick meal before being discovered. Nomadic lions, especially males and subadults, also enter resident pride territories as they follow the herds of buffalo and zebra.

The wet season in this part of Botswana generally only lasts from November to March, and the rains are often interspersed with long dry spells.

May and June are the critical months in the study area: the pans have mostly dried up, and the few that still contain water have been trampled and muddied by the last herds of elephant. The Okavango and its tributaries are the only source of water, and even though the rain began at the source in November, it often takes over six months to wind its way slowly through all the channels to reach this edge of the Delta. Predators survive well without water, taking what they need in fluids from their prey. The herbivores, however, are stressed without this vital liquid, especially since they are now grazing on grasses that are as dry as hay. Nutrition is there in abundance, but eating it only makes them increasingly thirsty. The browsers and mixed feeders like giraffe, impala, kudu, and

no discomfort to the animal, and the lions get used to wearing them in a matter of hours. The drug used to anaesthetise the lions is a combination of a dissociative anaesthetic and a sedative, which has been shown to be extremely safe and effective. The drug is injected using a lightweight plastic dart shot from a simple and silent gun using pressurised air. The vehicle is then moved away from the lion, and after 15 minutes a careful approach is made to determine the level of anaesthesia. The collar is then applied, a number of blood samples for disease and genetic analyses are drawn, and teeth and body measurements are taken. During the process, close watch is kept on body temperature, respiration, and heart rate, and noise is kept down to an absolute minimum. On completion of the handling, the vehicle is moved away, and the lion is carefully watched through binoculars to monitor recovery. This type of handling minimises stress to the animal, and ensures no future association of the vehicle with any negative experience.

Four neighbouring prides have been fitted with collars to date. These prides have been named after the areas they frequent, and are called the Santawani, Gomoti, Mogogelo, and South Pan prides. Every adult lion is named, as are cubs once they have reached one year of age. Younger cubs are given numbers for males and letters for females: thus S1, S2, SA, and SB would be male and female cubs of the Santawani pride. The members of each pride are shown in the table on page 9.

Below *Although solitary lions can have a whole kill to themselves, the advantages of group hunting are that they can catch much larger prey more often.*

eland can still extract moisture from their food, but the grazers have to migrate back into the wetter parts of the Delta. The pattern of abundance shifts again, and the cycle begins anew.

The Okavango lion research project

Our study requires that we find particular lions reliably. To this end, a pride male, two to three mature females, and one subadult male or female in each pride are fitted with radiocollars. These collars are lightweight and durable, have a battery life of about 34 months, and have a detection range of about 3 kilometres from the top of a vehicle. From the air, lions can be detected about 15 to 20 kilometres away, which becomes useful when tracking dispersing males. The collars cause

Each radiocollared lion is located at least once every two to three days. Even with the radiocollars, this is an arduous task. Our Land Rover dealer has probably never seen new vehicles depreciate faster, and our project is probably a major consumer of Maun's stocks of tyres, inner tubes, and patches. When radiocollared lions are eventually found, we note which other lions are present, where they are and how far they have moved from their last location, whether they have captured prey, and the habitat type in which they occur. Since lion pride members are almost never all together, and since group size and composition can change daily, it can take months before all the lions in a pride are known. Identification of individual lions is crucial, and is facilitated by noting their unique whisker patterns in combination with ear notches, nose

colour, black marks around the lower incisors, and body scars. The whisker pattern is composed of whisker spots above and below the top whisker row, and the number, size, and position of these whisker spots are unique to each lion. Because a relatively close approach is needed to identify lions by their whisker patterns, the process of identification can be quite frustrating at times, especially with lions that are new to the study area and shy of vehicles. We have often spent hours trying to get an accurate identification, inching the vehicle forward, and trying to peer through bushes and blades of grass to get the position of the last few whisker spots! Nevertheless, this time is well spent, as especially nomadic lions are not seen for up to eight or nine months at a time, but often pass through the area following migratory herds of prey.

Below Lions go to great lengths to avoid getting wet. At full stretch, one of the Mogogelo marsh lions leaps across a flooded pool ...

Identifying the lions enables us to recognise them individually, and thus allows us to get to know their characters. It is difficult to communicate the satisfaction we get from this, but each lion has an individual personality, and we truly miss them when we have to be away from the study area for any period of time. One cannot help empathising with their problems, mourn the loss of cubs, keep a concerned watch on animals that have been wounded, and laugh at the comedy of playing cubs and bumbled hunts. When one of the magnificent males of the Gomoti pride was found dead, the shock of seeing this beautiful animal reduced to scraps of skin and bone was profound and lasting. His death left a great void on the savanna, probably to the considerable relief of young males of the Mogogelo pride whom he regularly terrorised.

Similarly, the shooting of a nomadic lion for harassing a farmer's donkeys was deeply tragic. This scarred, one-eyed, embattled male had just reached the size and strength to challenge established pride males, and we silently cheered his efforts to become established in the Santawani area before he made the fatal mistake of crossing over the veterinary fence into a livestock zone. We miss subadults when they emigrate, and rejoice when a new litter of cubs is born.

In many ways, the passion that we feel for these lions also allows us to remain dispassionate. We do not pretend that they 'know' or 'recognise' us, we don't want to walk alongside them in the moonlight, treat their all too frequent wounds if these originate naturally (removal of a snare is another matter), or protect their vulnerable cubs when the

Below *... but miscalculates her landing.*

Right *The old Mogogelo female, Dolcetta, leads the way across the sodden floodplains.*

mothers have left them to go hunting. These are wild animals, and their wildness should be celebrated rather than tempered. We keep our interference in their lives down to a minimum and therefore decided long ago that information on hunting should not be collected by following groups of lions at night. While lions have been known to get used to and largely ignore a trailing vehicle, the same cannot be said for their prey. Following lions through the kinds of habitats present in the study area cannot be achieved without considerable noise and disturbance, and we limit observations of hunting to times when we find lions in open areas and can park the vehicle some distance away. While it would be fascinating to find out exactly how lions

hunt in forests, sufficient information can be pieced together from tracks after the hunt. Similarly, we have elected to keep visits to denning females down to the absolute minimum: once the den is located, we limit the visits to twice a week for ten minutes. Again, it would be riveting to know what mortality occurs among very young cubs, but the required disturbance is not worth the information.

In the next chapters, we will share our findings and our questions. Our aim is twofold: to better understand the way lions behave by combining observations in the field with information derived from use of advanced technology in the laboratory, and then to use this understanding to better guide conservation programmes.

Above *Crossing the flooded lagoons is a real problem for the lions. A young male snarls with irritation at this muddy prospect.*

Overleaf *In the confusion of a stampede, a zebra foal broke its leg and was immediately set upon. Greater numbers of lions have a better chance of capturing prey, but there is less to go round.*

Male lions

There is arguably no animal more evocative of Africa than a male lion. To begin to understand male lions better, one has to recognise that their behaviour and physical characteristics have resulted from a long history of evolution driven by sexual selection. Sexual selection is a form of natural selection, and directly rewards characteristics of the animal that enhance reproductive ability. Such characteristics either allow males greater access to females by being able to outcompete other males, or would reward males who are more attractive to females. A well-known example of the latter is the magnificent tail on a male peacock – female choice in this example has led to the evolution of a tail that is actually a severe encumbrance to the bearer.

To derive greater access to females by competition with other males, characters such as size and strength are usually rewarded by greater reproductive output. Male lions exhibit a level of sexual dimorphism (size differences among males and females of the species) that is unique among terrestrial carnivores. Rather than being fleet and nimble, selection has rewarded physical attributes that emphasise the necessary strength and power to challenge and fight off other males. Of course, there is a limit to such selection on size – while the biggest males may well be able to fight off smaller males, they cannot just keep getting larger. Male lion size is a compromise among many different selective forces acting on male morphology, including the basic necessity to pursue and capture prey.

Natural selection has also rewarded males that commit infanticide. Again, this behaviour has its origins in the depths of lion evolution, and is understandable only when female reproductive peculiarities are examined in concert with the short duration of pride male tenureship. Males come into their physical prime when they are about six years old, and it is only then that they can hope to challenge established pride males. If they are successful, they generally retain their tenure for about three years,

Opposite A nomadic male expropriated kills from Mogogelo females when Shiraz and Merlot were absent.

Above Perhaps aware of the absence of the three resident pride males, a coalition of three young Mogogelo lions trespass into the neighbouring Santawani territory, bravely announcing their presence by roaring together early one morning.

after which they begin losing physical condition. Cubs grow slowly and have a long period of dependence on their mothers and consequently female lions have a birth interval of about two years. Since pride males have such a short tenure, they must ensure that the females soon become reproductively receptive after they have taken over a pride. This is achieved by killing dependent cubs sired by the previous pride males: females who lose their cubs will mate again in a matter of a few weeks. Therefore, males who kill cubs are rewarded by reproductive benefits greatly in excess of males who wait until the cubs are grown. Infanticide is actually a rather common theme among a variety of species where males have a limited span of access to females with a long birth interval relative to male tenure.

There is much confusion, however, about the relationship between female oestrus and infanticide. Many guide books and scientific papers on lions will inform the readers that male lions commit infanticide to bring the females back into oestrus. For example, the *Behavior Guide to African Mammals* (p 371) unequivocally states that: 'Normally, lionesses produce cubs at intervals of no less than 2 years, and only come into estrus when their offspring are c. 1½ years old. The average interval between birth and the next estrus is 530 days. However, the loss of a litter causes a lioness to reenter estrus and mate within a few days or weeks.' The view that female lions do not come into oestrus for a considerable time after their cubs are born is now widely accepted, but is based on some very shaky foundations. Among domestic cats, for example, females come back into oestrus while their kittens are still unweaned, and there is no known physiological reason why female cats of any species should be different. Our observations indicate that female lions also come back into oestrus before their cubs are weaned, but avoid mating until their cubs have become reasonably capable of fending for themselves. Unlike domestic cat kittens, lion cubs have a long period of dependence on their mothers. It would thus be counterproductive for females to become pregnant too soon. Infanticidal males still need to kill cubs, not to bring females back into oestrus, but to change the behaviour of these females and make them more receptive to mating. We will discuss this further in the next chapter.

The wandering years

Male lions usually lead a short life fraught with danger. The arrival of new pride males and the abdication of their fathers too soon interrupts the early days of comfortable existence in the pride. Young males who are about two to three years old initially attempt to remain within their natal territory, but subadults unfortunate enough to be caught by new pride males are lucky to escape with considerable injuries. Also, the arrival of a new set of siblings causes the young males' mothers to be increasingly less tolerant of their presence. These subadults then become nomads and lead the lives of refugees, constantly being tormented as they trespass on established pride territories. In these days of reduced habitat, young males are frequently shot by farmers and ranchers when they resort to trespassing on agricultural land.

Baronne, a young male in the Mogogelo pride, must have established a record for his reluctance to leave his natal pride. We first found him in October 1995, when he appeared to be about two years old. He was usually in the presence of Zinfandel, but also associated with two slightly older males, Pinotage and Pinot Noir. In January 1996 Pinotage and Pinot Noir left the Mogogelo area and headed north, and initially Baronne stayed with them. By April he was back in the Mogogelo area, this time in the company of Vouvray, Grand Cru, Dolcetta, Riesling, and their nine six-month-old cubs. This association lasted until January 1998, when Baronne linked up with several different groups of subadult lions. He finally seemed ready to form his coalition and move on. Back to the Mogogelo females he went, however, and it was not until June 1998 that he finally moved out of the area with two other males. We next found him with one other young male about 40 kilometres to the west of the Mogogelo area, after which he tried to establish himself in the Chitabe area. There, he ran up

Above Shiraz expresses his rage at finding nomads in the Mogogelo pride's territory.

Opposite Sexual selection rewards physical attributes that emphasise strength and power to challenge and fight off other males.

area. Even though he was quite severely wounded on two occasions, this punishment did not seem to deter him. It was not until the Mogogelo pride was taken over by Yquem and Emilion that Baronne was finally persuaded to leave – he was then already more than four years old!

Nomadic males can travel large distances before they settle down. In Tanzania, a pair of males born in the Ngorongoro Crater made at least three trips to the Serengeti Plains and back again in successive years, a round trip distance exceeding 160 kilometres. In the Okavango, two males initially found with the Mogogelo pride (Pinotage and Pinot Noir) travelled at least 45 kilometres to the northeast before turning back again six months later. They stayed within the Mogogelo territory for another four months, and then headed northwest, last being found 35 kilometres from their initial starting place. A cohort of five males born to the Santawani pride initially headed 30 kilometres to the northeast, and then were last found 28 kilometres to the northwest of Santawani. Another single nomad found with the Mogogelo females (Inferno) completely disappeared from the area a few days after he was radiocollared, despite an aerial search covering 2 000 square kilometres. He then turned up a year later with three companions near the veterinary cordon fence, 17 kilometres from where he was collared. Since then, he has moved back into the study

Above Pride males give three-year-old males a hard time in their efforts to eject them from the pride. In ensuing skirmishes the young lions can suffer dreadful injuries.

against resident pride males and was killed in August 1999, about 20 kilometres from his natal area. His unwillingness to leave the natal pride was most likely increased by the lack of a regular presence of pride males in the area: Shiraz and Merlot split their time between the Mogogelo and Gomoti prides, and Baronne seemed to be successful at avoiding them when they were in the Mogogelo

Right Even though they may be unrelated, male lions in a coalition form strong and lasting bonds.

area, and has taken over the Gomoti pride. Finally, a coalition of two males was found in the Santawani territory in September 1997 (Gigondas and Gascoigne). Gigondas was radiocollared in December 1997, and these males roamed across the Santawani territory for two months, mating with at least one of the Santawani pride females (Chandon). In February 1998 these males left the area, heading for buffalo concentrations near the veterinary cordon fence. In March 1998 they must have crossed the cordon fence, because Gigondas was killed by residents of a village near Shorobe for attacking donkeys. At that point he was about 35 kilometres from where he was radiocollared.

The life of a dispersing group of males is as yet little understood, and needs considerable attention. Such dispersing males are critically important in the maintenance of gene flow between increasingly isolated populations of lions. We still have too little information to anwer even the most basic questions about the genetic structure of Botswana's lion pop-

ulations. Are they one large interbreeding unit, or have they historically existed as separate populations? Male lions in the central Kalahari, for example, are supposedly bigger and have darker manes than lions in the Okavango. Does this mean that Kalahari lions are genetically different from Okavango lions, or is this just local variation? If these lions are genetically different, then perhaps there has historically been no dispersal and gene flow between these populations. If they are not genetically different, then how can gene flow be maintained when dispersing lions are regularly shot as they traverse populated regions between the Okavango and the Kalahari?

Nomadic males are opportunists in every sense of the word. There is no necessity to patrol and protect a territory, and they are free to follow the migratory herds of buffalo, zebra and wildebeest. There is a widespread misconception that male lions do not hunt well, and certainly pride males will often appropriate kills from their females and

Above A young lion bites at thin air as he unsuccessfully lunges at a terrapin in a rain-filled pan. In time he will learn not to waste energy over this kind of fruitless pursuit.

other predators. Males might eventually grow too bulky to stalk and chase fleet antelope like impala and tsessebe, but they can be successful at capturing larger prey such as buffalo and zebra. These large herbivores form the mainstay of their diet during their nomadic phase, and the presence of nomadic coalitions is usually linked to the movements of migratory herbivores. Lions are also consummate scavengers, and nomads frequently gain free meals by taking kills from cheetahs, hyenas and wild dogs. Also, nomads will attach themselves to nomadic as well as pride females for a few days to weeks, depending on the vigilance of pride males, and will gain meals from accompanying such females on hunts. While they are with females, nomads display another form of opportunism involving reproduction. Nomadic males will mate

Right and Below *Lions are amazingly alert to vultures – when they descend they are immediately followed, even from distances of two or three kilometres.*

with females in oestrus when they come across them, and this includes those in established prides.

The few young males lucky enough to survive to maturity must then cope with the uncertainties of challenging established pride males. Usually young males leave their natal pride with others of about the same age, and stay together with these companions in male coalitions. There are definite advantages to forming coalitions: the Serengeti studies have shown that the chances of a single male obtaining tenure are about one in six. With two males, their chances improve to more than one in two, and three males together have a probability of over 90 per cent that they will be able to take over a pride and gain tenure. In addition, information gathered in the Serengeti has shown that larger coalitions of males father more surviving off-spring per male than do small coalitions. Young males who leave their natal pride alone or with a single companion can therefore benefit from forming partnerships with unrelated males to increase their chances of successfully taking over a pride. Even if young males leave with several companions, long-term studies have shown that initial companions are often lost and new ones found. Genetic analyses of Serengeti coalitions established that a high percentage of small breeding coalitions contained non-relatives.

Pride males

Eventually, a small percentage of nomads will become pride males. This has been described as the pinnacle of achievement for a male lion, but what are the advantages? Certainly pride males

Below Dispersing young males will often appropriate kills from other predators.

would seem to gain regular access to reproductive females, and by excluding other males from their territories, protect their reproductive investment and give their cubs a significant survival advantage. George Schaller mentions in passing the possibility that some males might remain permanent nomads, and there seems to be a case to be argued for males who choose not to become pride males. We are currently monitoring two adult males who seem to fit this category. Courvoisier and Armanac are two males in their prime who were first encountered in Chitabe, 15 kilometres to the west of the study area. We next found them at the southern extreme of the Santawani pride territory. The Santawani females chased them off, but a few weeks later they were found mating with two young females in the heart of the Santawani territory. They then mated with other young females in the South Pan territory, and were most recently seen deep in the Mogogelo pride area. Courvoisier and Armanac seem to have made the choice to traverse a variety of pride territories in the study area, opportunistically mating with oestral females along the way. These females are left to fend for themselves, but provided the pride males have had sexual encounters with them, they will accept the cubs as their own. There is currently not enough paternity information to determine the best strategy for adult males: take over a pride with all the inherent risks of injury or death, or remain nomadic and mate opportunistically.

There are other loose ends of male behaviour that need to be examined in greater detail. For example, the formation of coalitions, which at first gives males a significant advantage to successfully challenge established pride males, can also present them with some important reproductive difficulties. As coalitions get larger, the likelihood that any one particular male will be able to reproduce gets smaller. Some males, in fact, do not reproduce at all, and have been assumed to act as non-reproductive helpers to protect cubs. This would be fine among coalitions of relatives, as it makes evolutionary sense to protect related cubs. Assisting the reproductive efforts of close relatives occurs often in nature, and such altruistic acts are explained by invoking the concept of inclusive fitness. Individual fitness can be defined as the average number of offspring produced by individuals with a certain genotype, relative to the number of offspring produced by individuals with other genotypes. Inclusive fitness recognises that related individuals share genotypes, and therefore that you can

Right Flehmen: a Santawani male displays the involuntary grimace in response to oestrogen in a female's urine.

Above When these young males were hungry, tempers would flare over small kills. The females preferred to withdraw when fights became serious.

add to your own fitness by assisting the reproduction efforts of your relatives.

But what about coalitions that include unrelated males? Serengeti paternity studies have shown that partners have similar reproductive success in coalitions of two, but that a coalition of three could contain a non-reproducing partner. If this non-reproducing male is related to one of the reproducing males, all is not lost because he still has a measure of inclusive fitness. But if the non-reproducing male is unrelated, his defence of cubs is a waste of energy. The formation of a coalition thus becomes a serious liability for the unrelated individual. Later in this chapter we will also propose that even males who have grown up in the same pride might only be very distantly related. The inclusive fitness of an individual decreases rapidly as the degree of relatedness to other members of the group is reduced. The eminent geneticist J B S Haldane is supposed once to have said, 'I will gladly sacrifice my life for two brothers or eight first cousins': brothers share half of your genetic material, whereas cousins only share one-eighth. The bond formed among coalition partners may thus lead them to act at variance with genetic theories dealing with inclusive fitness.

The previous explanations as to why single males should team up with pairs of unrelated males are varied, but ultimately unsatisfactory (there are, of course, good reasons why a pair of related males should accept an unrelated third: chances are good that at least one of them will reproduce, and the additional partner will increase their chances of taking over a pride). The first explanation offered was that since females in a pride tend to come into oestrus simultaneously, mating opportunities would be equally distributed. In the Okavango, we observe that females actually come into oestrus at different times, and the available paternity information has already shown that reproductive success is skewed. It is true, however, that the male who first discovers and claims a female in oestrus will usually mate with her while his coalition mates wait in the wings. If these males are unrelated, such mating opportunities should be more hotly contested, but this is apparently not the case. The second explanation was that solitary males spend considerable time selecting companions, and will generally select companions who are younger and/or less vigorous. They thereby hedge their bets by accepting unrelated companions but still maintain their potential to breed. But are male lions really capable of sizing up their coalition mates and assessing their future reproductive potential? In the Santawani pride, it seems to have worked. A coalition of three males (Medoc, Mersault, and Montrachet) moved in after the original males (Beaujolais, Bordeaux, and Burgundy – aka the three Bs) abandoned the pride. The desertion of the Bs is discussed further below, but Medoc and Mersault are in their prime while Montrachet is much older and smaller. Surprisingly, Montrachet seems to have dominated most of the mating, even having to deal with two females competing for his attention while Medoc was lying close by. In the Gomoti pride, however, Inferno joined three younger males, and was largely excluded from the mating. Older males who join younger and stronger males in a coalition might sometimes win out: after all, they have had much previous experience, and the characteristics of the female lions' reproductive system could give them unexpected opportunities.

Clearly, much more work needs to be done with this dilemma of the solitary male.

Left *If a male wants any certainty of cub paternity, he has to mate with the female during her oesterus period.*

Moving on

When males take over a pride and mate with the females, their short tenure and the long inter-cub period would imply that the resulting cubs represent their lifelong reproductive achievement. It has been suggested that it would make much more sense from a reproductive point of view if males father cubs with a group of females, protect them while the cubs are vulnerable, and then move on to another pride. Observations made in the Serengeti suggest that cubs are substantially at risk from infanticidal males for approximately their first year of life. After that, the incidence of mortality among cubs drops off drastically: they have achieved the size and speed necessary to escape from strange males. This would seem to create a window of opportunity for pride males in that their full-time presence is no longer of the essence to ensure cub survival. They can now leave the cubs in the care of their mothers, and look for other reproductive opportunities. Pride abandonment has occurred in the Serengeti and in the Kruger, and the results there seem to satisfy predictions: males abandon cubs when they have reached a less vulnerable age, and then sire cubs with females of neighbouring prides. In the Okavango, the story is similar, but the consequences became more puzzling as

we continued to monitor the abandoned Santawani pride and followed the story to its conclusion.

The three original Santawani pride males (Bordeaux, Burgundy, and Beaujolais) took many exploratory journeys into neighbouring pride territories during their first 18 months of tenure. Also, they mated with females of the South Pan pride who entered the Santawani pride territory when prey availability in their own area was low. Once they knew the lay of the land, the presence of the three Bs dropped off sharply when their oldest cubs were about a year old, which is similar to the Serengeti observations. Initially, we had been able to find the Bs within the territory on more than 50 per cent of our attempts. Bordeaux, the radiocollared male, was with the pride females 30 per cent of the time, and often together with his coalition mates. After the older cubs reached a year in age, the Bs often spent over a month away from the Santawani females at a time, and our tracking success dropped down to about ten per cent.

Before they left, the Bs had mated with six of the eight pride females (the remaining two females were just reaching reproductive age), but after they abandoned the pride, they apparently mated with only one of seven reproductive females during their irregular return visits. Chandon even resisted mating attempts by the Bs, and instead mated with nomadic Gascoigne. Nomadic males, in fact, mated with four and possibly five of the Santawani females who came into oestrus, and two of these nomadic males have now taken over the Santawani territory.

Above Pride males often spend long periods away from the females, patrolling and marking their territory.

Opposite A distrustful stare from Bordeaux, one of the three large Santawani males.

Left Young males usually lead a short life fraught with danger. The arrival of new pride males and the abdication of their fathers too soon interrupts the early days of comfortable existence in the pride.

Above *To be confronted by the sheer ferocity of a dominant male is an intimidating experience – certainly frightening to a smaller subadult male.*

Opposite *Since Shiraz died in the Gomoti pride's territory his partner, Merlot, has faced an uncertain future.*

In addition, while the older cubs seemed safe from nomadic males, three litters of small cubs were lost. The three Bs are now left with only five cubs sired by them, and have lost at least eight cubs since they moved away. While it is true that the Bs have mated with two groups of females, the costs of the move in terms of loss of their own cubs and of guaranteed mating opportunities have been considerable.

The reason why males move on to seek additional mating partners could well be explained in part by the behaviour of pride females with dependent cubs. As mentioned above, females come back into oestrus soon after their cubs are born. Males are quick to detect oestrogen in the females' urine, and attempt to consort. However, females are not now receptive to mating and resist any advances made

by the males, sometimes to the point of aggression. Adult males should aim to maximise their mating opportunities during their limited reproductive life, and a lack of receptivity by their pride females should constitute a powerful incentive to cast their net more widely.

Males can occasionally hold two prides simultaneously, and thus gain access to a large number of reproducing females. In our study area, the Mogogelo and Gomoti prides were held by two imposing males, Shiraz and Merlot. Their visits to the pride females were correlated to seasonal prey availability in the two territories: during the wet season they mostly were with the Gomoti pride, but during the dry season, when prey availability dropped off in the Gomoti area, they spent consid-

erable time with the Mogogelo females. Their reception in the Mogogelo area was less than enthusiastic, and their appearance usually implied that the Mogogelo females disappeared from the area for two to three days at a time. Nomadic males were always a problem for Shiraz and Merlot, and they vented their ire on numerous occasions when they found such nomads in the Mogogelo pride territory. Their occasional visits, however, were sufficiently spaced to allow a diversity of nomads to attach themselves to the Mogogelo females, sometimes for weeks at a time. Their inattention also allowed Yquem and Emilion to mate with Zinfandel, and later move slowly into the Mogogelo area.

Yquem and Emilion provided a very interesting example of how little aggression can sometimes be involved when other males move into their territory. Yquem and Emilion established themselves in March 1998, but were soon faced with Haut-Brion and Hermitage, who were found nosing around the Mogogelo in June 1999.

Haut-Brion and Hermitage had their own group of females and 14- to 18-month-old cubs to the North in the Abaqao area, and their pressure on the Mogogelo males seemed to be applied in slow motion. This was all the more surprising as Emilion had broken his right hind leg in March 1999, and remained severely crippled. After three months of virtual residence in the Mogogelo pride area, Haut-Brion and Hermitage finally decided to make their move. The Mogogelo females were in oestrus in late September, and their scent was quickly picked up by Haut-Brion. Both males moved to where the females had been lying an hour before, and the smell of their oestrogen-laden urine evoked multiple flehmens (an involuntary grimace among both males and females in response to elevated oestrogen levels). Haut-Brion roared softly several times, and suddenly Yquem appeared on the scene, running at the intruders and roaring loudly. Yquem quickly realised the magnitude of the opposition, and ran off, chased by both males. They lost his scent after a few hundred metres, but quickly regrouped when Yquem gave away his location by roaring once again. They chased but did not find Yquem that night, and we found them sleeping off their exertions the next day. The following day, Haut-Brion and Hermitage were lying just across the river from the Mogogelo females, who eyed them suspiciously for about twenty minutes and then ran off with the cubs. Later that day, Emilion appeared at the river, and casually took a drink. We thought we would witness his last few minutes of life when Haut-Brion stealthily crossed the stream, and carefully approached the drinking lion. No more than five metres separated them when Emilion finally noticed him, and ran off as fast as his three legs could carry him. Haut-Brion took up the chase, and soon found Emilion standing in some palm scrub. He slowly approached Emilion, until they were again separated by a matter of a few metres. Instead of running off again, Emilion lay down. Haut-Brion stood over him, growled loudly ... and walked away. We had fully expected Haut-Brion to kill his crippled adversary, but instead witnessed something much more interesting – a choice to issue a warning rather than a death penalty. Emilion's submissive action probably played a major role in Haut-Brion's decision, as his attitude towards the more aggressive Yquem was radically different. Two months after these encounters

Opposite *A leopard returns to its impala kill hanging high in a rain-tree. Here it is safe from marauding hyenas.*

Left *Members of the lion genus Panthera have most likely evolved from solitary ancestors and all living relatives of lions – like tigers, jaguars and leopards – are solitary.*

Yquem and Emilion are still in residence, and Haut-Brion and Hermitage have retreated to their own territory.

Pride males remain opportunists. Like the nomads they once were, they continue to seek mating chances wherever they arise. They often make mistakes, and make decisions that with hindsight seem inappropriate. Certainly in areas where nomadic males abound, it would seem better to stay in close association with a single group of females rather than casting their net too widely. But this is precisely the point: there can be no definitives in nature, and since lions seem to be experimenting with sociality, their behaviour will continue to be confusing when compared with the ideal. A comparison with leopards could be useful in trying to interpret the behaviour of male lions. Male leopards have territories that include the home ranges of several females, and they attempt to exclude other males from access to these home ranges. Since lions and leopards most probably were derived from a common solitary ancestor, perhaps this acquisitional behaviour of female territories has persisted. Resident male lions might, therefore, attempt to take over as many neighboring female territories as possible, opting to hedge their bets in terms of missed mating opportunities. Such behaviour would not necessarily be selected against, because the reproductive rewards could occasionally be greater than if such males remained with a single pride. Since the Okavango study area is so seasonal regarding prey availability, and since nomads tend to follow migratory prey, the influx of nomads in this area might be higher than in other study sites. For example, a total of seven nomadic male groups has been observed in the Santawani pride territory during the past four months of the rainy season. This high influx of males simply cannot be controlled by pride males attempting to reside in two female territories simultaneously, nor can males who abandon prides expect to achieve high rates of cub survival in the face of such high alien male presence.

Male lion behaviour is flexible, and many preconceived notions should be abandoned. Males might spend a lot of time with pride females in some locations, but are noticeably absent in others. Two studies are revealing in this regard. First, male lions in the single population remaining in India are very rarely in the company of their pride females, except when females are in oestrus, or when a rare large animal has been killed. The Gir Forest is largely composed of dense vegetation, and males seem quite successful in stalking their own prey. Second, male lions in the Kalahari Desert similarly spent little time with their pride females, but often mated with females from different prides. It was suggested that reduced prey availability during the dry season coupled with small body size of the available prey contributed to this behaviour.

Trophy hunting and culling

Another situation in which male behaviour has shown some marked alterations has been noted among lion populations subjected to pressure from hunting or culling. Male lions, as stated earlier, are valuable trophy animals. In Botswana, hunting companies can sell a male lion to a client for sums exceeding US$30 000. Such is the demand for male lions that there is now an active breeding programme to supply private hunting areas in South Africa with 'trophy' animals, and there have been instances of captive male lions being transported long distances to game farms to be shot by 'hunters'. The Botswana Department of Wildlife

Right Receptive females exhibit pronounced sexual behaviour and actively seek out males.

and National Parks, acknowledging that little was known about the long-term effects of hunting on lion populations, gradually reduced the total lion quota from over 100 in 1988 to about 12 in 1998.

Lions have the distinction of being both highly desirable trophies and one of the most difficult animals to hunt sustainably. If pride males are shot in a hunting area, the consequent disruption to reproduction can be both dramatic and long-term. Incoming males will readily take over prides with missing defenders, but in doing so will kill cubs belonging to the previous males. Consistent hunting pressure on pride males will thus interfere with the reproductive potential of prides in hunting areas. It would seem best to target post-reproductive males and possibly nomads as trophies, but that requires individual identification and a high familiarity with the males in each hunting area. Even the selection of nomads can have long-term effects on natural levels of turnover among males.

Studies of male lions in areas with high hunting pressures have shown some interesting results. In the Kruger National Park in South Africa, lions used to be regularly cropped to ameliorate conditions for populations of prey species. In Kruger cases were observed of males accepting additional partners after they had joined prides and females

Above The lioness begins a flirtatious courtship which ends with her lying down in front of the chosen male in a classic mating posture.

cobbling together prides composed of survivors. A similar observation was made in the Luangwa Valley of Zambia, where high hunting pressure resulted in a severely depleted male lion population. Males, as mentioned, generally form coalitions before they take over a pride, and have not been observed to accept additional companions once they are resident. In male-depopulated areas, however, their flexible social system allows them to make such alterations, presumably to improve their chances of maintaining tenure.

Mating

Male lion copulatory endurance is impressive. It has even been proposed that this has resulted from selection of ever-increased sexual stamina: females could thereby evaluate not only the male's endurance, but also get an overall impression of his vigour. Such strong males would be more likely to be able to fend off competitors and defend cubs. Numbers quoted on male reproductive behaviour are often quite staggering: they are supposed to have copulated about 3 000 times for every cub that survives to a year in age, mating with lionesses for three to four days, and averaging one copulation every 20 minutes or so. Sometimes, males copulate at a very fast rate, and we have recorded copulations once every 10 to 15 minutes. Such persistence and endurance is doubtless impressive, but is hardly necessary from a reproductive point of view. While sperm concentration in lion ejaculates has not been measured as a function of time, the level must drop off rather quickly after the first several ejaculations.

Sperm are made by processes of cell division within the testes and take considerable time to accumulate. Concentrations of sperm are most likely highest in the first few ejaculations, and then probably decrease to low or non-existent levels during the remainder of mating activity. Since the first copulations are necessary to induce ovulation in the female, it would seem that the best quality ejacu-

Opposite *Males often bite the necks of their mating partners during copulation.*

Below *It only makes evolutionary sense for non-reproducing males to protect cubs if these males share a genetic relationship with other members of their coalition.*

lates are wasted. Sperm can remain viable for about 24 hours, however, and eggs are probably fertilised by sperm from those early copulations. So why then this long-term association between mating males and females?

Experiments with domestic cats have shown that more queens become pregnant after multiple copulations than if the tom is removed after a single copulation. So while there is a benefit to multiple copulations, three to four days of copulatory activity still seems excessive! We feel that this long-term copulatory activity does not necessarily serve a reproductive function, but constitutes a 'fail-safe' activity by the males. In fact, this long-term association is probably regulated by female rather than male behaviour. Females in oestrus exhibit pronounced sexual behaviour and actively seek out males nearby. On numerous occasions we have seen females moving towards roaring males, and they actively advertise their oestrus by urine marking. Simply put, when females are in oestrus, they will demand mating (except when they have cubs, which we will discuss later). If a male abandons a female after he has mated with her but while she is still in oestrus, she will seek out another male with whom to copulate. We have even seen instances when females have shifted over to other males in attendance when the mating activity of her original partner has dropped off. Basically, if a male wants to guarantee that all cubs resulting from a mating bout are actually his, he will have to keep the

Above This is the most common attitude that lions are found in: sleeping under bushes. Exposing their bellies in this way helps to keep them cooler.

Opposite After a cold winter's night the lions are active well into the late morning.

Opposite Many prey species are only seasonally present in the Delta and the lions must make do with small resident antelope like lechwe.

Below As the young males grow survival becomes tougher for the younger females, one of whom tries desperately to hang on to her share of a kill.

female at his side by mating with her during her entire oestrus period. The male's limited sperm supply also plays a role in his need to closely guard a female during her oestrus. Other males often remain in proximity to a mating couple, and if the mating male's sperm supply has been exhausted in bringing about ovulation, then a fresh supply from a waiting male will have a high probability of impregnating the female. A male has to mate with a female throughout her oestrus: even if he stands little chance of getting her pregnant, at least he is preventing other males from sneaking in and being rewarded with paternity!

A corollary of such long mating periods is that sperm concentration in a particular male's ejaculates are likely to remain low for a considerable time afterwards. If a male comes across another oestrous female shortly after mating, his chances of impregnating her are probably quite low. The failure to get pregnant has usually been ascribed to the females, but it might well be the fragility of the males' reproductive system that is responsible.

Paternity

The Serengeti studies have indicated that pride males sired all the cubs in the pride. This has been widely quoted as convincing evidence of the benefits to the risks male lions take when they acquire prides. In the Okavango, however, we have considerable observational evidence that cubs might not always be related to the pride males. In the Santawani pride, for example, one of the females mated with Bordeaux while other females in the pride mated with Medoc and Montrachet, who had just become established. Remember that the original Santawani males abandoned the Santawani pride, and

Above Bordeaux tolerates the curiosity of a small cub. There is no way for him to know if he has fathered this cub or whether it belongs to one of the other males in his coalition, a previous pride male, or even a nomadic male.

moved north to take over the neighbouring South Pan pride. Similarly, one of the Mogogelo pride females, Vouvray, mated with the previously resident males, Shiraz and Merlot, before that pride was taken over by new males. The initial period of confusion during takeovers is probably a time when such litters of diverse paternity appear, and in both cases, the new males have accepted the cubs as their own.

This all adds up to a much more complicated pattern of relationships among members of a pride than previously supposed, especially when the additional complexity of unrelated coalition males is factored in. It is possible, for example, to have cubs in a pride that have as fathers one of the previous pride males, one of the current pride males, and another of the current pride males who is unrelated to the first. From a genetic point of view, the cubs in the pride can therefore have a very low level of relatedness to each other, especially if their own mothers have a similarly distant genetic relationship. There is another interesting corollary: the

cubs belonging to the female in the Santawani pride who mated with Bordeaux are in fact more closely related (half siblings) to the cubs in the South Pan pride than to the other cubs in their own pride (cousins at best if their mothers are full sisters). This is becoming complicated, but nevertheless fascinating. Even males from the same cohort growing up in the same pride might have very little genetic relatedness, and the same is true for the female cohorts. If these females are subsequently recruited into the pride, it might be conceivable that very distantly related pride-mates end up defending their territory against more closely related individuals from a neighbouring pride.

Why is this so interesting? In short, cooperative behaviour and altruism among group members used to be one of the major puzzles in evolutionary biology. Since selection acts on the individual, the behaviour of that individual should promote its own reproductive success. Altruism, or commonly observed behaviours that could jeopardise an individual's survival or reproductive potential while benefiting others, does not seem to fit a Darwinian perspective. Darwin himself admitted that altruism 'at first seemed ... fatal to my whole theory'. With a better understanding of genetics, however, the dilemma was seemingly explained by invoking kinship. If members of your group are related to you genetically, it makes evolutionary sense to feed them, defend them, and even forego your own reproductive chances to improve those of relatives in your group. Similar actions that involve non-relatives make no sense evolutionarily, since you are wasting resources or your own reproductive potential to further the interests of strangers. If you die to save your brother's child, at least some of your genes will survive to the next generation. The more distant the relative, the more you should hesitate to take this course. If you die to save a stranger's child, you are committing evolutionary suicide.

We have already seen that it makes no evolutionary sense for an unrelated male to defend cubs sired by other males in his coalition. But how does the same situation work for females in a pride if the cubs are also only very distantly related? Is group membership among lions in actual fact more important than kinship? And if so, can the lack of a more conventional sociality among lions be explained by the lack of straightforward genetic relationships among members of a pride? We will address some of these questions in the next chapter.

Left *A red lechwe throws up cascades of water as it races into the swamps, its refuge from predators.*

Top *The pangolin is an insectivore and has survived unchanged for millions of years ...*

Above *... after 20 minutes of trying to bite his way into the pangolin's armour the lion gives up, leaving the creature no worse for its experience.*

Left *The lion is perplexed as the pangolin rolls itself into an armour-plated ball ...*

Female lions

Lion society is matrilineal, and therefore female lions form the core of the pride. Females in a pride have usually been proposed to be related to each other as a jumble of nieces, cousins, sisters, aunts, and grandmothers. This may be true in some instances, but as we explained in the previous chapter, there are good reasons to suppose that the story may well be more complicated. Nevertheless, the pride territory belongs to the females, and where long-term studies have been done, these territories have remained stable over decades. Female lions are therefore responsible for the continuity of prides, and their reproductive success determines to a very large extent the presence of lion populations in a given area.

The number of females in a pride can vary tremendously, and as many as 18 females have been reported as belonging to a single pride. Habitat and prey density govern pride size and in the Okavango the average pride contains about six females. Pride

females have definite preferences for female companions. This preference is perhaps most evident when females are not joined to protect their common offspring, but even when females have young cubs, they associate most frequently with preferred companions. In the Gomoti pride, for example, Margeaux and Gamay are almost always together; in the Mogogelo pride Vouvray and Grand Cru, Dolcetta and Riesling, and Zinfandel and Retsina generally form pairs. These preferences seem to be determined by compatibility, although membership in a natal cohort also seems to play a part.

Females born into a pride either stay with that pride for the rest of their lives or emigrate. Female emigration has not received much study, but some interesting facts are known. In the Serengeti study, most young females emigrated before the age of four years. The causes of such emigration include a takeover of their natal pride by new males, avoidance of breeding with their fathers if they matured in the presence of their fathers' coalition, or disper-

Opposite Cubs stay with their maternal group much longer than any other cat species and can unite lionesses into tight-knit groups during this dependent stage.

Above The pride's cubs are united in a crèche and suckled jointly.

sal when their mothers give birth to a new litter of cubs. The largest percentage of young females did not emigrate, but joined their mothers' prides, a situation described for the Santawani pride in the previous chapter.

Emigrants either left the area completely, or established new prides peripheral to their native pride. Such peripheral females either rejoined the pride when they came into oestrus after the arrival of new males, or established independent prides with males of their own. These new prides either established ranges that were wholly within their original prides' ranges, adjacent to and overlapping those ranges, or represented a subdivision of the original prides' ranges. Emigrant females who left their natal prides sometimes roamed considerable distances before settling down next door. In the Serengeti, young females who left their natal prides

took longer to have cubs and lived shorter lives than those who stayed: there was thus a 'cost' to dispersing. Inclusion of young females in their natal pride also seems to depend on the number of adult females already present. If females are born into small prides, their inclusion is usually possible as it is when prey density in the pride area increases. Females born into large prides have less chance of inclusion.

The Serengeti studies, however, leave two questions unanswered. First, while an initial batch of young females might be able to split off from their natal pride and settle next door, this cannot go on indefinitely. Pride territories cannot continue to be subdivided. Second, what happens to the females who completely leave their natal area? In the Serengeti, no new females joined the pride, although this has happened in the Okavango and

Below These tiny cubs are born completely helpless and mortality can be high during the early weeks. Mothers will often leave these defenceless cubs for periods of up to 24 hours while they hunt.

Left *The tiny cubs remain in the security of their den for the first months of their life. As cubs grow and become more mobile, dens are abandoned but females continue to hide cubs under bushes and shrubs.*

Below *A rare picture of a newly-born cub taken with a long lens. Females with very small cubs are highly susceptible to stress, and visits to dens can adversely affect cub survival. After this picture was taken, the den was not approached for six weeks.*

the Kalahari. We have seen a number of nomadic groups consisting of mixtures of young males and females form short-term associations with existing prides, only to move on later. Young male lions all leave their natal prides, enter a nomadic phase, and either die or eventually become pride males. Some young lionesses probably also become nomads, but what is their fate? Some of them might successfully establish prides distant from their natal areas, some of them probably become problem animals and are shot, but the fate of dispersing females remains an open area in lion research.

Why do female lions form groups?

We have probably all heard the phrase 'she was like a lioness protecting her cubs' when mothers rise to the defence of their children. In actual fact, lionesses are such bad mothers that it is sometimes surprising that the species has survived to this day. Shortly after the completely defenceless cubs are born, their mothers leave them in the den when they go hunting. These absences can be prolonged, and females have been recorded to leave their cubs for up to 24 hours. Because lion cubs grow slowly,

Above Animals like the eland attain a body size that renders them immune to predation by all except lions.

Opposite The lionesses spend an exhausting day defending the carcass against dozens of vultures.

such absences by their mothers are a relatively constant feature of their early lives. Even when cubs are joined in crèches, females do not delegate babysitters to look after their offspring as is the case among other predators like African wild dogs, and it is little wonder that cub mortality is high. Young cubs are practically defenceless against a diversity of potential threats to their lives from hyenas, leopards, and even jackals. When times are tough, females readily exclude cubs from feeding at kills, and will abandon them when food becomes truly scarce. Cub mortality, as a result, can be very high: in the Serengeti, 67 per cent of cubs did not survive their first two years of life in the 1960s, and 86 per cent did not reach the age of two in the 1970s. In a sense, lost cubs are relatively easy to replace because of the short gestation period of female lions, but it still surprises us how perfunctory maternal care can be. A good example of this recently occurred with Lancon, a young female in the Gomoti pride. Four cubs were born in her first litter, and survived well for their first eight weeks. Lancon then decided to join the other pride females and their eight-month-old cubs. The older cubs enthusiastically suckled Lancon, depleting her supply of milk. Lancon compounded her mistake by taking her small cubs on

some long-distance hunts with the rest of the pride. During one of these long journeys she lost two of her cubs, one of whom managed to find and join Santawani pride females Amarula and Sancerre and their nine cubs. There seemed to be no problem with acceptance of the cub, but because Amarula and Sancerre's milk had dried up they could not adequately feed the small stranger. After five days, she was eventually left behind once again, and we have not seen her since. It is interesting to speculate about the possible course of events if Amarula and Sancerre had still been lactating: would Lancon's cub have become a member of the Santawani pride?

Defence of cubs has been proposed as one of the main reasons why females form prides. Previous studies estimated that mortality as a result of infanticide accounts for more than a quarter of all cub deaths. Females who joined together in groups, however, were more successful in cub defence than single females. Cub mortality due to infanticide was thus proposed as a powerful selective force to unite females in defensive alliances. Experiments were performed to lend indirect support to this hypothesis: taped roars of single females and groups of three females were played to nomadic males and their responses noted. In most cases, males would approach a single female roaring, but were either hesitant or withdrew when a chorus of three was played to them.

There are of course a diversity of selective factors that would favour group formation of females, but it is interesting that defence of cubs from potentially infanticidal males has been proposed as one such factor, especially when defence of cubs from other sources of mortality is rather lackadaisical. In fact, it would seem that females would do better to address the other more significant sources of mortality among cubs (75 per cent or more of cubs that die do so from starvation, abandonment, or 'unknown' causes where cubs have disappeared from the pride between one observation period and the next) before dealing with the occasional infanticidal male.

A group of females can, however, be extremely effective in showing off male lions. Recently, the Santawani pride killed a giraffe at the southeastern border of their territory. One of the pride males, Medoc, was present, but more interested in Amarula than in the carcass. When we came upon the kill, Chandon, Sauvignon, Cabernet, Asti, Moet, and their 11 cubs were feeding, and had been joined by Clicquot, who, like Amarula, was preg-

nant. As we looked around, we noticed two strange males lying nearby: old boys with full black manes and yellowed teeth. Everyone seemed relaxed, but as the males got up, they were immediately set upon by all seven females. One of the males was lucky enough to make good his escape, but the other was at one point buried under five snarling and biting females. We thought he would surely be killed, but with a supreme effort he managed to throw them off and run into the mopane forest. Belatedly, Medoc took up the chase, but limited his efforts to a show of roaring.

The next time we saw these two males, the situation was even more astounding. By now, we had named them Courvoisier and Armanac, since they were regularly seen in the Santawani area. The Santawani pride had killed an adult male buffalo; and five females, 11 cubs, and one of the pride males were on the kill. As we drove up, we noticed another male sharing the kill, and to our amazement it turned out to be Armanac! Montrachet, the Santawani pride male, and Armanac were feeding side by side, and the females were eating from the opposite side of the carcass. The cubs darted in and out, at times feeding right next to Armanac. There was no more aggression than is usually seen among lions at a kill, and as the carcass was consumed, Montrachet was more concerned with keeping the females away than taking any action against Armanac. On one occasion the females tried to see

Armanac off, but he merely stood up and growled, which was sufficient to elicit a rapid retreat. When only scraps remained the females and cubs ambled off, followed a short time later by Montrachet. Armanac gnawed a few bones, drank at a pan, and then wandered off in the opposite direction.

Is the threat of infanticidal males sufficient to join female lions together in groups? Infanticide is known to occur among tigers, leopards, and pumas, whose females nonetheless remain solitary. Although it is often stated that lions are the only felid species that has social females, feral domestic cats often form matrilineal female groups. Such sociality could not have been influenced by the need to protect kittens from infanticidal males, because infanticide has not been recorded among domestic cats. In fact, while grouping among female lions might lead to better cub protection, it cannot explain why lions became social.

Another proposed reason why females unite in groups has to do with defence of territory. Since females pass their territories on to successive generations, a high level of familiarity with territory boundaries is built up among female pride-mates. Where long-term studies have been done, such territories have remained stable for generations, with relatively minor shifts in boundaries. Also, females presumably build up long-term knowledge of the most productive hunting areas, which in the Okavango region vary considerably from season to

Left Females are extremely aware of oestrus cycles among other females in their group. Like males, females exhibit an involuntary grimace when they detect elevated levels of oestrogen in the urine of one of their companions.

Opposite The young lions imitate their elders by sharpening their claws on the same tree that the adults have just used.

Above One of the lionesses of the South Pan pride, Chenin, calls her cubs from the nearby den to a zebra she had just killed.

Opposite above Sitting on top of the carcass the tiny lion tastes blood for the first time.

Opposite below The two six-week-old cubs had never seen a carcass before and explored the dead zebra with enthusiasm.

season. Our studies have shown that females can predictably be located in different parts of their range depending on wet or dry season prey availability. However, they also gain a good knowledge of their neighbours' territories when they trespass in search of prey, and there is considerable overlap in territories when yearly movements of prides are mapped out. Like other researchers, however, we have found that there are some parts of the pride territory that are not trespassed on by neighbouring lions, and these have been called core areas. These core areas are where lions in a particular pride focus most of their activity, and as a result trespassers would stand a high chance of being detected.

Detection of trespassers from a neighbouring pride by resident females is rarely an aggressive event. On most occasions, trespassers enter a pride territory for a short period of time before returning to their own territories. Even when they manage to make a kill in a neighbouring territory, they have usually retreated again by the next morning. When trespassers are detected by resident females, howev-

er, the interaction generally consists of more sound than fury. One incident occurred when females of the resident Santawani pride discovered Mogogelo pride trespassers on a zebra kill. The initial aggression, in fact, was directed to the residents by the trespassers, and the residents only became aggressive when the single lingering adult female finally left the kill. The five Santawani females attacked the lone Mogogelo female, but backed off when she rolled on her back and snarled at them. She was eventually allowed to walk off unmolested.

On another occasion, three Santawani females with their cubs came upon two trespassing South Pan females. After staring at the trespassers for about five minutes, Amarula rushed at them, closely followed by Sauvignon. Cabernet did not participate, and led the five yearling cubs off in another direction. After much snarling and roaring, the trespassers walked off, and Amarula and Sauvignon rejoined Cabernet and the cubs. All encounters we have witnessed, in fact, have consisted of skirmishes rather than battles, and no lion has been wound-

ed in any of the encounters between neighbouring pride females.

The relative lack of aggression in defence of territories might well have to do with the abundance of prey in the Okavango area: since there is a risk involved in aggressively challenging trespassers in search of prey, it might be better to let them eat their fill and move on. As we will explain later, it could also be explained by significant levels of familiarity among females of neighbouring prides.

Defence of territory, however, has also been proposed as a significant selective factor in the formation of groups among female lions. Certainly, a single female would stand little chance against a group of neighbours in defending her territory, and information from the Serengeti indicates that females in very small prides are unable to defend permanent territories. But this hypothesis is rather like the chicken-and-egg question. Which came first, sociality among females or the ability to better defend territories as a company? Territorial defence, like cub defence, is more likely to have

Right *Zinfandel, one of the collared lions, was just as comfortable to go it alone. Despite being a member of the Mogogelo pride she spent very little time with them.*

Below *As the dry season tightens its grip, the herds begin to arrive in those parts of Moremi flooded by the Okavango.*

been a secondary benefit, albeit one that reinforced the perhaps tenuous initial groupings of female lions. Proponents of the importance of territorial defence as a reason why female lions live in groups have stated that lions live at higher densities than any of the other large cats. Such high population density could lead to the shared defence of territory, as suggested for bird species. But do lions really live in higher densities than other large cats? The solitary leopard is a significantly understudied species, but some researchers have proposed higher densities of leopards than lions in areas where both species occur. In the Kruger National Park, for example, the average male leopard territory measured 100 square kilometres, and included three to four female territories. An average lion territory of 300 square kilometres could therefore include 9 to 12 adult female and 3 adult male leopards. Such

densities are probably higher than the number of adult lions found in a territory of that size, so the density/shared defence of territory/sociality argument is compromised.

A third proposal as to why females form groups has to do with procuring food. Lions were hypothesised to be ideal subjects for studies on grouping because they live in fission-fusion societies that allow members to form subgroups of various sizes. This would allow testing of 'optimal' foraging predictions. In fact, based on limited and probably inappropriate data from Serengeti lions, it was proposed that individuals hunting in groups of two would gain the highest rate of food intake. Solitary lions would of course have the entire kill to themselves, but were less efficient at capturing prey than when they had help. More than one helper, however, meant that food had to be increasingly shared: a greater number of hunting lions would have better success at capturing prey, but then there would be less food to go around. Lions, however, rarely hunted in groups of two, and a number of explanations were offered to mitigate the discrepancy.

A more thorough analysis of food intake was then conducted, and it appeared that during times of food scarcity, single females and groups of four or more actually fared better than groups of two. Females in small prides remained in the largest possible group size, presumably to better defend territories against neighbours. Also, females with dependent cubs gathered in groups at variance with optimal foraging predictions. The study once again concluded that defence of territory and cubs was more important than the advantages of group hunting in explaining why females form prides. But as we have seen, these are arguments weakened by comparisons with other solitary and social felids.

So why are female lions social? Or rather, why are they social to the extent that they are? As stated, defence of cubs and territory are probably secondary benefits that reinforced an initial alliance. We believe the initial alliance was formed because of the advantages of hunting in groups. Other researchers have rejected this possibility because single females were observed to achieve a feeding success comparable to that of females hunting in groups. This is a weak argument, and it is much more constructive to look at the development of sociality among females from an evolutionary point of view.

The African savannas abound with a diversity of very big herbivores. Adults of these potential prey

Above A lioness, Vourray, who has hidden away her two three-month-old cubs fathered by a previous pride male, actually engages in a mating bout with a new pride male in the Mogogelo territory.

animals attain impressive body sizes and weights: buffalo weigh in excess of 500 kg, eland about the same, and giraffe about 1 000 kg. While lions are the largest of the diverse array of predators in Africa, no single lion is able to tackle adults of such large prey. Competition for medium-sized animals like impala, gazelle, reedbuck, bushbuck and warthog is intense: they are preyed on by a wide selection of predators like cheetahs, African wild dogs, leopards and hyenas as well as lions. The enormous food resource represented by large prey animals would therefore go unutilised unless large predators like lions joined together in groups. Apart from a limited amount of competition from group-hunting hyenas, this resource is exclusively available to lions. Joining together in hunting groups thus has immediate selective benefits, which could then be augmented by benefits that accrue from jointly suckling and defending cubs, jointly defending territories, etc.

Selection on large size in a predator is not without costs. Lions are not capable of great speed, fast turns or endurance races. With large prey like buffalo and giraffe this is not particularly necessary, but when hunting fleet animals like zebra, wildebeest, tsessebe and kudu, a large predator can compensate for lack of speed by using stealth and a group strategy. Hunting will be discussed in greater detail in the next chapter, but it is easy to visualise the benefits of group hunting to large predators. On the one hand, it allows them to take down some of the largest animals in the herbivore community, and on the other, it allows them to compensate for the handicap of their large size to prey on animals much faster and more nimble than they are.

Does the fact that female lions are successful in solitary hunts exclude the possibility that procurement of food was a strong factor in the evolution of their sociality? Other social carnivores such as wolves, coyotes and hyenas are also successful when they hunt alone, and solitary hunting is much more an indication of flexibility and adaptability than an argument against the advantages of group formation. In the Okavango, when large migratory prey like zebra, buffalo and wildebeest are scarce, females not joined together by the need to care for cubs often become solitary hunters. The availability of cover in the form of woodlands and floodplains with dense sage bushes allows single females to stalk smaller prey like impala and warthog successfully. In more open habitats like the Etosha in Namibia, a single lion would hardly stand a chance of capturing vigilant prey. Success in solitary hunting therefore depends on factors like the relative availability of small and large prey as well as the kind of habitat lions use for hunting.

Sexual behaviour and motherhood

As mentioned before, female lions are induced ovulators. With this system of reproduction females require the stimulus of mating to trigger ovulation. In the absence of mating, there is no ovulation, and females can rapidly come back into oestrus. Induced ovulation is very cost-effective and evolved especially among solitary species or those with rapidly maturing young. As we mentioned in the Introduction, lions inherited this method of reproduction from their ancestors, but they do not qualify either as solitary or as having young that need minimal care. Their system of reproduction has presented lions with many problems, which they have resolved reasonably well. Nevertheless, their reproductive behaviours have been significantly misinterpreted.

Let us give you some examples. It is often stated that after losing their cubs in a takeover, female lions mate for about four months without becoming pregnant. During this time, they supposedly engage in 'heightened sexual activity', seeking out many partners and copulating frequently. Sexual stamina, it is thought, is perceived by females as a reliable indicator of the capability of males to hold

the pride against future challenges by other coalitions. Therefore, by assessing the endurance of males, female lions 'ensure' the future presence of a coalition that will protect their reproductive investment. A number of hypotheses have been put forward to explain this four-month period of infertility: it has been proposed to be an 'adaptation' that protects females from desertion by the new males; it helps bond new males to the pride; or it allows time for the strongest male coalition to discover and take over the pride. This all sounds plausible, but such hypotheses actually reveal an astounding level of ignorance about underlying mechanisms. How can females mate but develop a 'strategy' to keep themselves from becoming pregnant? These observations, rather than being interpreted as an 'adaptation' or 'strategy' that benefits females by securing the best possible males for the pride, can be interpreted much more realistically with an understanding of reproductive hormones and the lions' oestrus cycle.

As stated before, the oestrogen produced in the early stages of a female's oestrus cycle primes her reproductive system to respond to the stimulus of mating. When males take over a new pride, they stick to their newly acquired females like glue, and begin mating at the first sign of oestrus. If the female's reproductive system has not had sufficient time to be effectively primed when mating begins

Below Relationships among pride females and new males are often uncomfortable after a takeover.

Opposite top *Eight-week-old cubs of the South Pan pride.*

Opposite below *A tender moment as one of the younger lionesses in the pride shows her fascination with her young relative.*

Below *Lions may suffer dreadful injuries when hunting. This gash was caused by the sharp flailing hooves of a kudu bull, killed the previous day. In time the wound will heal and, within the pride, she will survive.*

she will take much longer to ovulate. By that time, the male's supply of sperm has been spent. Only when the males gain confidence in their tenure and become less domineering does the system have any chance of working.

It might also be important to consider the effects of stress hormones. Elevated levels of stress among female lions might be expected when new males take over a pride, or when nomadic males come into the pride territory. A pride takeover involves quite aggressive behaviour by the males towards the females, especially if females try to protect offspring sired by the previous males. Female lions are quite often wounded during these encounters, and there have been reports of females being killed when they are particularly vociferous in defence of their cubs. Elevated stress hormone levels in these situations can interfere with the production of luteinising hormone. This means that females will come into oestrus normally, but if there is no production of luteinising hormone, these females will not ovulate. Therefore, instead of postulating that

females employ a delayed ovulation strategy to ensure the long-term interest of new males and the eventual tenure of the strongest coalition, it is much more probable that stressed females fail to ovulate for several oestrus cycles. This stress-related delay in ovulation might achieve the same end, but it can hardly be termed a 'strategy'!

Similarly, some observers have suggested that females already pregnant before the arrival of aspirant pride males go through an apparent oestrus and mate with the new males. Such behaviour had previously been observed in primates, and is thought to have the function of 'fooling' males into believing that cubs born subsequently are their own, and thus protect them from infanticide. We do not believe in 'apparent' oestrus – hormonally, a female is either producing elevated levels of oestrogen or she is not. A more convincing explanation for this observation involves the production of elevated levels of oestrogen towards the end of pregnancy. This surge of oestrogen is necessary to prime the reproductive system in the anticipation of

birth. This oestrogen peak, however, may be detected by males in the area, who will respond as if the female is in oestrus.

The females show little interest in males at this time, and rebuff them time and again as they try to copulate. However, some persistent males do occasionally succeed. Since male lions cannot count, cubs produced a matter of weeks after copulation will still be accepted as their own. Once again, complex reproductive strategies were invoked to explain an observation whereas a better understanding of lions' reproductive systems provides a much simpler and more convincing answer.

A lion female's birth interval is variable, but usually those who have raised cubs successfully do not mate again until the cubs are between 18 months and two years old. Contrast this with domestic cats, who take the much more traditional induced ovula-

tor 'conveyor belt' approach to reproduction and mate again even before their kittens are weaned. Indeed there is evidence that induced ovulators continue to produce follicles during pregnancy. Lion cubs stay with their maternal group much longer than the young of any other cat species. They grow slowly, have much to learn from the adult females, and do not attain any level of independence until they are about two years old. The survival of these cubs would be severely impacted if their mothers became pregnant again too soon. In the previous chapter, we mentioned that it has now become widely accepted that female lions do not go back into oestrus for about 18 months after their cubs are born. No mechanism was proposed to explain this period of anoestrus, and our observations show that female lions actually come back into oestrus soon after their cubs are born. Clearly, a better understanding of oestrus is required.

Oestrogen (derived from the Greek word *estrus* meaning 'sexual frenzy') is a key reproductive hormone, but whatever the Greeks lead us to believe, oestrogen is not simply a 'sex potion'. Its influence is far reaching and multi-faceted, and many neural pathways are stimulated by the presence of oestrogen. Bearing this in mind, there is not likely to be an inhibitory mechanism to stop the production of this hormone. While we have seen pronounced sexual behaviour among females in oestrus, these same females can also be strongly disinclined to mate at other times. Females thus seem capable of behaviourally overriding their hormonal messages when they have dependent cubs. We base this statement on two pieces of evidence. First, Kate Nicholls, who is primarily responsible for the lion reproductive work in this project, initiated studies of reproductive hormone levels among females by collecting faecal samples. This study, in collaboration with Dr Janine Brown of the US National Zoological Park Conservation and Research Center, indicated that there was a good correlation between presence of female reproductive hormone metabolites in faecal samples and reproductive behaviour. Janine had earlier established that oestrus cycles could be accurately monitored among captive felids by analysing faecal samples, and our sampling confirmed that this non-invasive method could be used to monitor free-ranging lions as well. Second, we established a strong relationship between the presence of oestrogens and certain behaviours. By smelling each others' genitals and urine, lions are able to continually

Left These cubs, brought to an eland kill for their first experience of fresh meat, seem uncertain what to do with it and end up playing on the carcass.

Right *High above the long grass, a lioness's precarious perch under a raintree offers her a good vantage point to observe prey.*

assess each other's reproductive status. The presence of elevated levels of oestrogen elicits flehmen. By monitoring the females regularly over many months a clear pattern emerged: females' urine elicited flehmen at intervals corresponding to the usual oestrus cycles. There is a good correlation between elevated levels of oestrogen in the faecal samples and the occurrence of flehmen.

If female lions do begin regular oestrus cycles soon after the cubs are born, what then prevents these females from becoming pregnant while they still have highly dependent cubs? Kate has shown that the answer lies in female behaviour. First, we have documented that females with dependent cubs become very intolerant of the pride males, especially when they are in oestrus. They regularly march up to the males and force them to move, and often cuff them if they do not comply. On one occasion, Medoc was able to sneak up on Moet during a rain storm and tried to push her down and mount her, but she vigorously rebuffed him and ran for the protection of the other Santawani females. Despite

Below left *Her hilarious efforts to get down are not the normal dignified behaviour associated with a lioness.*

Below right *In contrast, the leopard shows great confidence in its agility in trees.*

this treatment the males will try to stick close to females who smell so interesting, but do not seem to get the chance to mate, especially when females are in a group. Single females with cubs can be overpowered and mated, but such mating bouts are of much shorter duration than when females are receptive and therefore do not stimulate ovulation. We have not observed females with cubs mating for more than a day, although Schaller mentions that one female with young cubs copulated for two days. Second, females with cubs also seem to avoid males by frequenting little-used parts of their territory. We have observed this behaviour for females of the Santawani, Mogogelo, and Gomoti prides, but this strategy is not always successful – the males usually find them in the end, in which case the females again resort to intolerant behaviour.

With this scenario, infanticide of cubs by incoming males takes on a different perspective. As stated in the chapter on males, infanticide of very young cubs might well serve to bring females back into oestrus. Females with older cubs are likely

already experiencing oestrus cycles, but unwilling to mate as long as they have dependent cubs. Infanticide of those cubs is necessary to change female behaviour, but comes at a cost – females whose cubs have been killed are not likely to be immediately receptive of the new males, and this could explain the often significant time lag between the takeover of a pride and birth of cubs.

Flexible bonds and ties of convenience

Associations among female lions are usually quite consistent when they have young cubs, but pride females often reshuffle themselves when the cubs are old enough to be independent. Individual females then peel off when they come into oestrus and are mated, leaving the responsibility of their offspring to the remaining females. Eventually, subadults are often left in the care of one or two females. If this care coincides with a changeover in pride males, these grown cubs can become a liability to the female left in charge. Such females and their dependants are no longer safe in their own pride territory due to the aggressive reception by the new males. Similarly, they are not welcome in adjoining territories. These guardian females usually stick to the fringes of their territory, actively avoiding any contact with the males. Occasionally,

Opposite left Sauvignon returns an obstinate six-week-old cub to the den.

Above left One year old and the games have become rougher.

Left and Above right Two years later, they have grown into healthy young lions who still enjoy each other's company.

they will join their pride mates at large kills, but never in the presence of the unwelcome juveniles. If these fringe groups do encounter the pride males, the females may be severely wounded while protecting the adolescent cubs.

Membership in these fringe groups changes over the years. In both the Santawani and Mogogelo prides, females have reshuffled after their prides have been taken over. For example, in the Santawani pride, Chandon took care of nine subadults when Amarula, Sauvignon and Cabernet gave birth to new cubs. Bordeaux, Burgundy, and Beaujolais were very aggressive towards these subadults, but tolerated Chandon. Only when the five subadult males emigrated and the four young females came into their initial oestrus did Chandon once again become a regular member of the pride. Then it was Amarula's turn to take care of the subadults and try to avoid the new pride males, Medoc and Montrachet. Dolcetta's story is even more interesting. She formed a core breeding group in the Mogogelo pride with Vouvray, Grand Cru, and Riesling. She and Riesling then headed north with the cubs when the Mogogelo pride was taken

Above and right *The cubs' constant demands for attention are not always appreciated by other members of the pride.*

Opposite *Play is an important part of any young creature's education. Not only does it form bonds, but the games reflect more serious aspects of adult behaviour that will ultimately be essential for their survival.*

Above *In an extraordinary display of teamwork, three lions link up in mid-air.*

over by Yquem and Emilion. Riesling rejoined the Mogogelo pride after an absence of about a year, and has recently given birth to two cubs. Dolcetta and two females from the Mogogelo litters born in 1995 have also spent considerable time in the company of females and males of the Abaqao pride. Dolcetta seems to be flitting between these two prides, and it will be fascinating to see where she settles.

The relationship between the Mogogelo and the Abaqao prides is a very interesting one, and has led us to believe in the concept of a superpride. Remember that both these prides live in an area of very high prey density even at the height of the dry season. Cub survival to dispersal age has been close to 80 per cent, and is likely to have been as high in previous years. If subadult females settle nearby their natal prides, the current females in these two groups could have a high degree of familiarity with each other. Encounters among members of these

two groups are frequent, and we have seen members of both groups feeding from the same carcass. Retsina joined the Mogogelo pride as a core group adult breeding female, even though we had not seen her since the beginning of the study. Dolcetta is as comfortable with the Abaqao females as with the Mogogelo females. Our current thinking is that the Abaqao and Mogogelo prides form a pool of females who split into groups due to a variety of circumstances. Core groups in both assemblages divide as grown cubs split off with some females while others begin breeding again. New core groups are formed when new males arrive on the scene and carve breeding groups out of the pool. Group membership is therefore largely determined by the pride males.

Another important aspect of male behaviour that affects females is their tendency to form coalitions of unrelated individuals. This, together with the fact that females can be mated by males of the previous coalition just before others take over, can potentially result in prides that contain only very distantly related cubs. Indeed, genetic relationships might even be closer among cubs living in neighbouring prides if their fathers have shifted next door. This kind of complexity of genetic relationships among lions can wreak havoc with traditional explanations of cooperation and altruism based on kinship. It is therefore not that surprising that observations have been made of females hanging back from others during territorial conflicts, and other females not willingly participating with others in hunts that could involve danger of injury or mortality. While lions form groups, these groups are ultimately composed of individuals. Such individuals might have formed strong bonds because they have grown up together, but this does not mean that females will cooperate to the extent

encountered in more closely related groups of other social animals. Selection might well favour the lioness who propagates her own genes in a pride consisting of very distantly related animals, and thus rewards 'cheaters' who do not participate in potentially dangerous activities. Sociality can therefore be compromised, and while there are benefits to associating in groups, these are sometimes likely to be jeopardised by the advantages of acting in one's own benefit.

The common thread running through several chapters in this book is 'why are lions social?' We have explained that lions are very likely to have evolved from solitary ancestors, and, indeed, all of the large cat species living today – with the exception of lions – are solitary. Lions lack many of the characteristics of other social animals, females are saddled with a reproductive system that makes more sense for solitary cats, and while they join in groups,

Below Yearlings of both sexes respond to heightened oestrogen levels by engaging in sexual behaviour towards females.

Opposite top Lionesses form fission-fusion groups in which members can change daily. It is only on rare occasions, like on large kills, that all members of a pride come together.

Below Amarula's small cub attracted a lot of interest from the older cubs who were warned several times not to get too close.

Following page At six weeks the cubs are inquisitive and love to explore their surroundings.

seem as comfortable to go it alone. The question that can be asked is therefore 'are lions moving towards greater sociality, moving away from sociality, or likely to remain static in their current system of group living without being social?' All we have to work with is their initial starting point (probably not social) and their current status (not very social).

From a genetic point of view, we have discussed the variety of ways in which relatedness among individuals in a group of lions can be severely reduced. In this situation, kinship can no longer be called upon to maintain the ties that bind, and individuals now recognise each other as kin mainly because of their association with each other rather than because of their genetic relationships. This erosion of genetic relatedness came about because of a selective loophole in the formation of male coalitions: joining together in a group of unrelated individuals made the acquisition of prides easier. Once unrelated males begin breeding with pride females, the relatedness of cubs in successive generations is greatly reduced. A succession of closely related male coalitions taking over the pride might swing the pendulum back towards greater relatedness among cubs, and one would eventually end up with a situation in which some prides are composed of close relatives, some composed of individuals of intermediate levels of relationship, and some composed of individuals with hardly any relationship to each other at all. The deciding factor in the types of relationships to be found in any area would be the ratio of male coalitions composed of non-relatives to male coalitions composed of close relatives. This ratio could vary from generation to generation: high cub mortality in a given year would lead to formation of more coalitions composed of non-relatives, whereas high survivorship would promote the formation of more coalitions of relatives. Heavy trophy hunting could also play a part: nomadic male coalitions could be expected to be made up of more non-relatives in areas where there is consistent hunting pressure on males.

Genetic relationships among cubs can decrease very quickly, and this is best illustrated with an example. In the figure opposite, two unrelated males mate with four females genetically related to each other by 15%, an average value reported in the literature. Eight cubs result from these matings. Cub a is related to cub b by 50 per cent (full siblings). Cubs a and b are related to cubs c and d by 29 per cent (half siblings with an additional contribution because their mothers are related). Cubs a, b, c and d are related to the other four cubs by only 4 per cent (no genetic relatedness between the fathers, and a small contribution from their mothers). In the next generation, female cubs b, d, f and h grow up and are recruited into the pride. They again mate with two unrelated males, and again produce eight cubs. The relationship between cubs a and b is 50 per cent as before, the relationship between cubs a and b, and c and d is 32 per cent (half siblings with a greater contribution because their mothers are more related than in the first generation), but now cubs a, b, c and d are only related to cubs e, f, g and h by a level of 1 per cent (no genetic relationship between their fathers, and a much smaller level of relatedness between their mothers than before. In this scenario, two generations of mating with unrelated males has resulted in cubs that are genetically virtual strangers living in the same pride.

Another important factor in the reduction of levels of genetic relatedness in prides is the lack of a social hierarchy among lion males and females. As long as breeding is shared by most individuals, the result will be a pool of cubs of mixed relationship. If strong social bonds are best reinforced by close kinship, lions will always remain loosely social as long as males continue to form mixed coalitions without a dominance hierarchy. The most likely answer to the question posed above, therefore, is that lions are probably now as social as they ever were, and are not likely to become more social in the absence of behavioural changes. The notion of directed evolution went out a long time ago, and animals are sets of compromises to a diversity of selective pressures. They either do well with what they have, or suffer the consequence of extinction. In the absence of any serious competitor, lions will continue to muddle along, even with their strange social system.

GENETIC RELATIONSHIPS

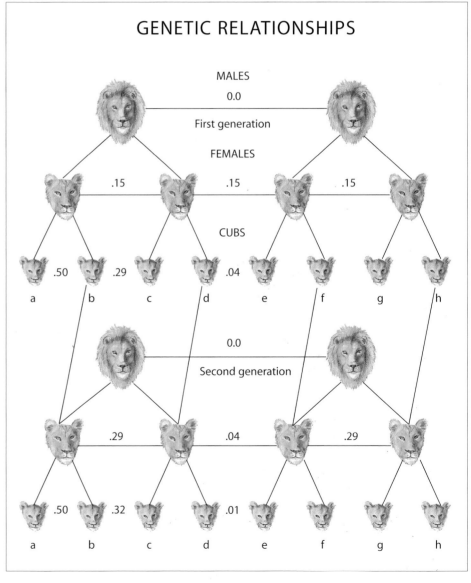

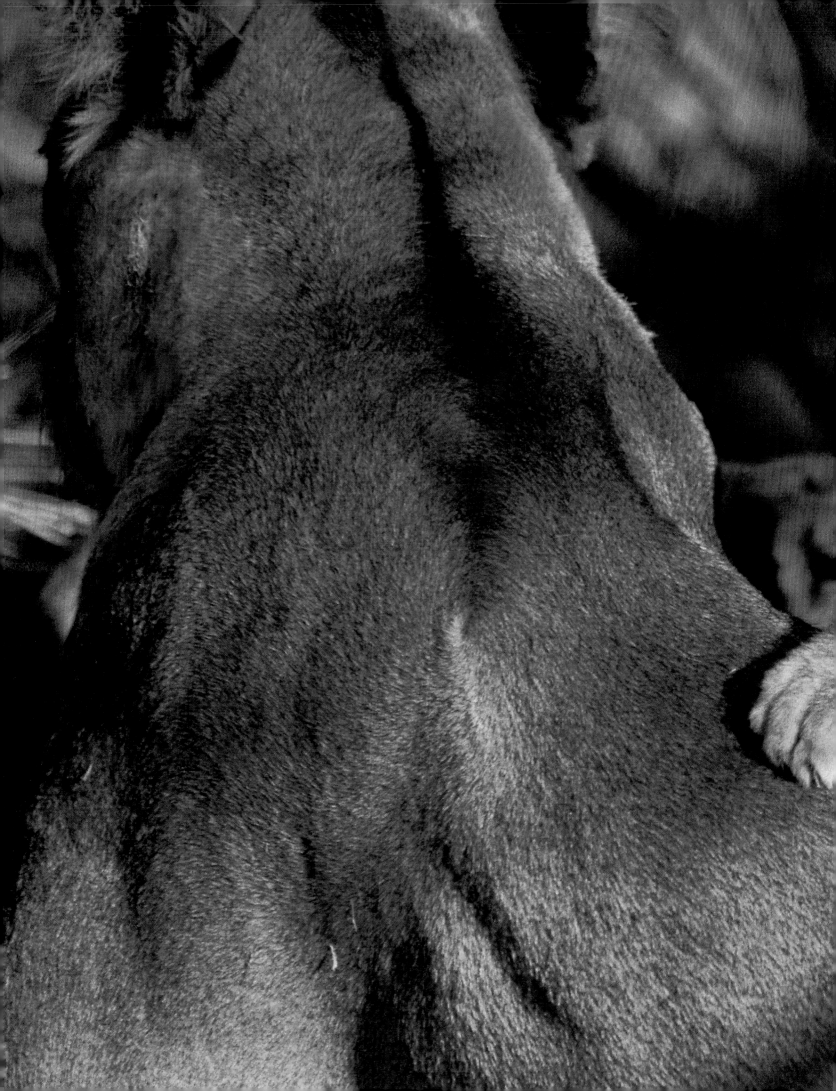

Hunting

Lions are the largest of African predators, and because they often hunt in groups, can probably be called the most formidable living carnivore. This is not to say, however, that they have an easy time acquiring their meals: just as predators have evolved to hunt, so their prey has evolved to avoid and evade predators. A successful hunt for lions is dependent on speed, strength, stealth, teamwork, opportunity ... and luck. Strategies vary with prey type, and a hunt for buffalo proceeds along very different lines than a hunt for impala or warthog. Given that lions hunt a much greater diversity of prey animals than other African predators, their repertoire of hunting strategies is therefore much more extensive than that of carnivores like African wild dogs, leopards or cheetahs.

We are fascinated by predators, and much of this captivation stems from the excitement of the hunt. George Schaller, who studied lions in the Serengeti for three years from 1966 to 1969, found observing a hunt 'a moment of almost unbearable tension, a drama in which it was impossible not to participate emotionally, knowing that the death of a being hung in the balance ... from the lion's point of view [this activity] is more important than any other in its day-to-day existence'. This preoccupation with observing hunting has persisted, and there is now a considerable volume of literature detailing how lions catch their prey.

To some degree the hunt has become romanticised: lions are 'shadows in the grass', silently stalking their unsuspecting prey with deft movements that would be the envy of famous strategists like Shaka Zulu and George Patton. Particularly difficult prey is trapped with adroit pincer movements, or carefully guided towards strategically placed lions lying in ambush. In group hunts, some individuals always take the left flank while others prefer the right; other lions, mindful of the danger of flying hooves or sharp horns, lag behind until the prey is caught and then rush in to claim their share. In fact, lions generally have low success rates given

Opposite The Mogogelo pride have learned that treed baboons rarely remain in their safe perches: when a lion makes a rush up the base of the tree they panic and leap to the ground, where they are easily caught.

Above A study in power, but lions are not capable of great speed, fast turns or endurance races.

Above *During the hot dry months, the Mogogelo lions use the dense reedbeds around the marsh to lie in wait for thirsty animals coming to drink.*

Above right *Warthogs are mostly hunted by a solitary lion, even if a number of other pride members are present. Not blessed with good eyesight, warthogs are generally caught after a careful stalk and sudden rush.*

Opposite top left *Dolcetta chases the warthog onto uneven ground on a dry lagoon bed where it stumbles and is caught by Riesling rushing in.*

Opposite top right *The warthog is quickly overwhelmed under the weight of the two lions.*

Opposite below *Lions are often clumsy killers and their prey can suffer a long and agonising death. It takes seven minutes for the warthog to die.*

average prey densities, and while we have seen numerous attempts by hunting females to outflank their prey, many a wrong move is made and the prey usually escapes before the trap is sprung. More often than not, lions make baffling choices of direction – diametrically opposite to concentrations of prey – when they set out to hunt. Similarly, we have witnessed countless occasions when unsuspecting prey animals have walked within seemingly easy range of a group of hungry lions, who have done no more than flatten themselves in the grass and watch as their meal walked off. On the other hand, these same lions may become extremely efficient and catch three or four buffaloes in a single night, and always appear fat and healthy even under conditions of very low prey density. As always, lions can only be predicted to be enigmatic!

The outcome of any hunt is as much dependent on the response of the prey as the efforts of the lions. As mentioned, selection has favoured those prey animals able to escape predation, and herbivores are well endowed with the speed and senses necessary to avoid being eaten. Zebra, wildebeest, tsessebe, impala, warthog, giraffe and buffalo can all run faster and longer than lions, and their senses of sight, smell and hearing are at least equal to those of their predators. Added to this, predator avoidance was probably a key factor in the evolution of sociality among large prey animals, most of which live in herds. Many eyes, ears and noses are better able to detect danger, and all herding animals have developed visual or auditory warnings to

alert others in their group to predators. Behaviour also plays a role. Prey animals avoid areas of dense cover, or are very vigilant when in positions of potential danger, like when they are approaching water. Most animals drink in the daytime, and prefer to rest in open areas. Night vision of animals such as impala, tsessebe, wildebeest and zebra is in all likelihood equal to that of their predators.

With all these factors stacked against them, predators must make many attempts to catch their prey, and successful hunts usually involve prey that become confused and make mistakes, or that are handicapped by age, poor condition, disease or injuries. That predators like lions only remove the old, sick, or weak members of their prey populations is a misconception, however. Predators are opportunists, and will take advantage of any chance they get. A healthy animal running the wrong way is at greater risk than a crippled animal making the correct choice, but a weakened animal that cannot keep up with its fleeing companions is more likely to be singled out by hunters. An examination of prey animals successfully captured by lions might therefore show a preponderance of very young and old individuals, but conclusions drawn from such lists are often muddled by the presence of a substantial number of animals in their prime.

Lions are quick to take advantage of animals stressed by environmental conditions. This is perhaps most noticeable in a strongly seasonal environment like the Okavango, where periods of drought are more the norm than wet years. A long

Above Prey animals, like this tsessebe, try to avoid the lions by running parallel to the river, but when the lions spring their trap correctly they are cut off and brought down. That is the theory – but in practice the lions often make incredible mistakes.

Right Undetected by a herd of wallowing elephants, the lions watch for an opportunity to grab an unsuspecting calf.

dry season can last up to nine months, and even the most water-independent herbivore will lose condition under these circumstances. We have never observed lions attacking giraffes in the rainy season when these animals are in prime condition, although the simultaneous presence of wildebeest and zebra might divert their attention. Larger numbers of tsessebe are killed in the dry season, and these animals are usually classed as the fastest and most alert of all ungulates. Perhaps most convincing, however, is that we have only recorded lions killing subadult elephants in the dry season, especially towards the end of this period when conditions are most desperate. At this time, elephants travel long distances between sources of water and food, and lose condition rapidly. Apart from calves separated from their herds, healthy elephants are seemingly immune to predation: their strength and size are sufficient to deter even the most determined predator, and their thick skins are exceedingly difficult to bite through. Many elephants die during the dry season, however, and weakened and dying animals can be tackled with greater ease.

Hunting techniques and choices

Part of the long dependence of lion cubs on their mothers has to do with their demanding apprenticeship. The Okavango lions have to date been recorded as hunting 19 different prey animals, ranging in size from springhare to giraffe and elephant. Obviously, a wide variety of hunting techniques are required for this number of prey species. Warthogs, for example, are most often hunted by a solitary lion even if a number of other pride mates are present. They are generally caught after a careful stalk and a sudden rush, but some warthogs seem almost oblivious to their surroundings, and often one will blunder into a group of resting lions. Nimble impalas require a group hunt to maximise chances of capture, but solitary lions frequently

Above *Unsuspecting animals walk within seemingly easy range of a group of lions who do no more than watch as the prey walks away.*

Right *Nimble impalas are often caught when they are preoccupied during the rutting season.*

Opposite above *A large predator must compensate for lack of speed by using stealth or a group strategy.*

Opposite below *Once an impala is driven onto uneven ground by the marsh it loses its advantage and is often caught by the other lions lying in wait.*

capture preoccupied impala males during the mating season. Most impalas are brought down by sweeping them off their feet, and killed by a hold on the neck.

All the larger prey animals are killed only by groups of lions, but strategies differ. Zebra and wildebeest are usually captured when there are enough lions to execute flanking movements. Zebras maintain a dense herd when they are running from predators, and young animals are shielded in the middle of the fleeing group. A zebra is most often caught by a lion jumping on its back or grabbing the haunches; once it is brought down, the attacker will shift hold to the neck. Wildebeest dodge and zigzag, and even run sideways with their heads facing the attacker. They too are usually

Right *The Mogogelo lions were very successful at catching impala, often in preference to larger, more dangerous prey.*

Below *Young lions do not seem to be immediately able to apply the skills learned in play — they depend entirely on the adults for food.*

Opposite above & below *Cubs will often play games involving sticks, balls of elephant dung or the tail of an adult.*

overpowered from behind. With buffalo, the lions make little attempt to remain hidden, and preferentially target stragglers bringing up the rear of moving herds. The lions' approach is to create panic in the herd, and then cut out solitary individuals. Buffalo hunts can take considerable time and perseverance, as the herd will often rally to defend a surrounded or wounded individual, and some buffaloes take hours to kill.

When hunting giraffe, lions again rely on panicking their intended victim, and do not make any attempt to stalk. Because of their size, giraffe are difficult prey, and can only be brought down if they can be chased over broken ground or through a strip of forest with fallen trees. Once the giraffe falls or stumbles, the combined weight of the lions is sufficient to overpower the animal.

Complicating the task of mastering this diversity of hunting techniques is the fact that many prey animals are only seasonally present within any given pride's home range. This would mean, given that lion cubs are usually about 8 to 10 months old before they take any attentive interest in the hunt, that they will not have experienced the full range of prey hunting strategies until they are at least 18 months old.

Play of young lions has been assumed to sharpen their hunting skills, and many aspects of play are similar to the techniques they will use later in life to capture prey. Cubs will stalk others using cover, or lie in ambush waiting for other cubs to walk by. From a very early age, they are able to knock other cubs over by sweeping their feet out from behind, or catch them by jumping on their backs and grabbing a hold on the nape of the neck. Cubs frequently wrestle, with one cub lying on its back and the other trying to grab it by its throat. They will stalk ground-dwelling birds like francolin and guinea fowl, and play games with sticks, balls of elephant dung, or the adults' tails.

As they grow, cubs will play with adults, jumping against their sides or trying to catch legs. Adults will also play with cubs, either holding them down with their paws and gently biting them, or chasing them and knocking them over. Older cubs sometimes target younger cubs and chase, bite and grapple with them. Such playfulness tends to decrease as the cubs grow older, although we have witnessed extended periods of chasing and grappling among three-year old females in the cool of the evening or after rains, and occasionally, adult females wrestle and try to trip each other up. Young males are in general less playful than females, and we have never observed any play among adult males.

This convergence of patterns of play and hunting techniques has led many behavioural biologists to propose a functional role for play among young carnivores. Play among cubs is likely to have an important role in developing coordination, strength and neural integration, but does it have a functional role? As noted by Schaller, cubs only play in the comforting presence of their mothers, and become quiescent when left unattended. Also, Schaller made the important point that young lions mainly learn the intricacies of stalking and killing prey by trial and error, and by watching adults. They do not seem to be immediately able to apply the skills learned by playing to capturing prey. Seen in this light, play among young lions might well be construed as a means of strengthening social bonds, and it is therefore not surprising that the incidence of play drops off as lions age. Also, the young of many cat species have remarkably similar ways of playing: kittens, cheetah cubs and lion cubs all play in basically the same way, although their eventual methods of prey capture are quite different.

Pride preferences and seasonal availability of prey

While the Okavango lions have been recorded hunting 19 prey animals to date, this is not to say that cubs have to learn how to hunt all of them. Each pride may show distinct preferences, and this is no more evident than when comparing the neighbouring Santawani and Mogogelo prides. In order of decreasing percentages, the Mogogelo pride's top four prey species are warthog, impala, baboon and zebra. The Santawani pride, on the other hand, has most success with giraffe, buffalo, impala and zebra. The Mogogelo pride has a per-

Left The Mogogelo pride also jump baboons when they are drinking, trapping them against pools along the marsh. While not much of a meal, they are relatively easy to catch.

Right *The baboon's valiant attempt to intimidate the lioness fails and she grabs him in a deadly embrace – then suffocates him with a throat grip.*

Below *A young male, uncertain how to dispatch his victim, sat for some minutes with a squealing baboon in his jaws.*

manent river within its territory while the Santawani pride only has water in seasonal pans, but this cannot account for these major differences. Baboons occur in abundance in the Santawani pride territory, but we have never seen the Santawani lions make any attempt to hunt them. In one instance, the Santawani pride was walking under a tree full of baboons when one baboon lost its grip and fell from a high perch, killing itself in the process. The lions merely sniffed at its body before walking on. While the Santawani lions have stalked warthogs, they have never been successful at catching them. Similarly, giraffes are plentiful in the Mogogelo pride territory, but the lions there show little interest in hunting them. When their prey animals are compared, an overall pattern emerges: the Santawani lions usually kill large animals, while the Mogogelo pride mainly kill smaller ones.

The observation that the Mogogelo pride kill so many baboons was surprising. Lions have been recorded as killing baboons in areas like Lake Manyara in Tanzania, but the Mogogelo pride seem to have brought it to a fine art. Though baboons can easily take refuge in trees, the Mogogelo lions have learned that they rarely remain in their safe perches, but panic and leap to the ground to get away, especially when one of the younger lions makes a rush up the tree trunk. Once on the ground, however, they are easily caught by the waiting lions. The Mogogelo pride also jump baboons when they are drinking and become easily trapped against pools in the river. While a baboon is not much of a meal, these lions have learned that they are relatively easy to catch.

Learning thus plays an important part in the kinds of prey caught by each pride. Cubs growing up in the Mogogelo pride will have learned how to successfully hunt baboons and warthogs, but will not know how to hunt a giraffe. On the other hand, cubs in the Santawani pride do not seem to have any idea that baboons are edible. It is very possible that techniques learned as cubs will persist for life, and that the preferences of a particular pride will endure for generations.

Another important difference between the neighbouring Santawani and Mogogelo prides pertains to the time of day these lions hunt. Lions are usually thought of as nocturnal hunters who only occasion-ally make kills during the day. This is certainly true of the Santawani pride, who rarely move from the shade of their resting places except on cold winter days. The Mogogelo pride, however, hunt primarily by day even at the hottest time of year. We believe the difference is almost entirely explicable by the presence of permanent water in the Mogogelo pride territory (although again, learned behaviour is likely to play a part). Literally hundreds of wildebeest, zebra, tsessebe, impala and warthog come from kilometres away to drink, and try to minimise the risk of predation by drinking during the day. The favourite hunting strategy of the Mogogelo lions is to conceal themselves in tall grass or behind bushes close to the water, wait for their prey to come to the river to drink, and then rush out of concealment. Prey animals generally try to escape by running parallel to the river, but when the lions spring their trap correctly, they are cut off and brought down. Or at least, that is the theory: in practice, the lions can often make incredible mistakes.

Below Lions find the fur of baboons distasteful and prefer to pluck it out before feeding.

Following pages Lions are quick to take advantage of animals stressed by environmental conditions and this is most noticeable in a strongly seasonal environment like the Okavango, where periods of drought are more common than wet years.

Right *Warthogs seem almost oblivious to their surroundings and will often blunder into groups of resting lions.*

Below *The outcome of a hunt is as much dependent on the efforts of the lions as the response of the prey.*

Opposite *The eyes of a stalking lion, transfixed on its quarry.*

We once witnessed a desperate impala trying to leap over the river, but it was caught in mid-air by a pursuing lioness. Both crashed into the water, and the lioness swam to the opposite bank. Nineteen lions of various ages hesitated for a few minutes on both banks watching the struggling impala before they summoned the courage to enter the water. In their usual frenzy to feed, the lions managed to push the hapless impala under the water and into the muddy river bottom. Confused about the disappearance of their meal, they plunged about in the mud, pushing the impala ever deeper into the river bottom. Wet, bedraggled and filthy, the pride crawled onto the banks to dry out and try again.

On another occasion, a lone lioness lying in some reeds meticulously stalked a warthog drinking at the river. By flattening herself on the ground she managed to get within about 10 metres of the warthog, which suddenly looked up, spotted her

and trotted off. After a few seconds, however, the warthog seemed to forget what it had seen, and returned to drink at exactly the same spot. The lioness, who had remained immobile, was now presented with a second chance, but her seemingly half-hearted rush allowed the warthog to make an easy escape.

That the Okavango lions hunt 19 prey species is rather unusual compared to lions in other parts of Africa. Also unusual is the lack of a clear numerical dominance of any particular prey species in their diet, or even the lack of dominance of a group of prey species. With most other lion populations studied, three or four species will make up at least 75 per cent of the lions' diet. For example, in the Serengeti (Seronera), lions eat mostly zebra, wildebeest and gazelle. In Lake Manyara National Park, their preferred prey are zebra, impala and buffalo. In Kafue National Park in Zambia, buffalo,

PREY TAKEN BY THE SANTAWANI AND MOGOGELO PRIDES

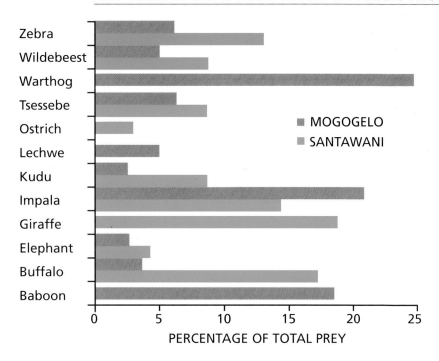

Zebra
Wildebeest
Warthog
Tsessebe
Ostrich
Lechwe
Kudu
Impala
Giraffe
Elephant
Buffalo
Baboon

■ MOGOGELO
■ SANTAWANI

PERCENTAGE OF TOTAL PREY

PERCENTAGES OF PREY KILLED BY OKAVANGO LIONS

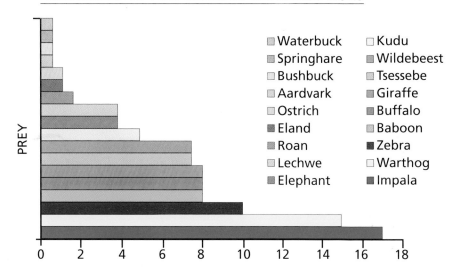

PREY

□ Waterbuck   □ Kudu
■ Springhare   ■ Wildebeest
□ Bushbuck   □ Tsessebe
■ Aardvark   ■ Giraffe
□ Ostrich   ■ Buffalo
■ Eland   ■ Baboon
■ Roan   ■ Zebra
□ Lechwe   □ Warthog
■ Elephant   ■ Impala

tsessebe, warthog and zebra constitute most of the lions' kills. In the Okavango, however, lions seem much more catholic in their diet, and the percentages of eight prey species (impala, warthog, zebra, baboon, buffalo, giraffe, tsessebe and wildebeest) have to be totalled to add up to a figure near 75 per cent. We believe the difference is largely due to the strong seasonal aspect to prey availability. The lions in the Okavango study area can only hunt buffalo, zebra and wildebeest for five to six months of the year, during the wet season, and then have to make do with the water-independent species. This seasonality to prey availability, as mentioned, requires a considerable diversity of hunting strategies.

Sight, sound and smell

A predator's senses play a very important part in the ability to detect prey. As humans, our surroundings are perceived mainly by vision, and as a result, we live in a sensually deprived world. We cannot even begin to appreciate the diversity of smells and sounds that make up a lion's world, and even though we are able to distinguish more shades of colour than most animals, we sacrifice night vision for colour vision. At night, our vision is mainly monochromatic, even when there is a full moon. And because the colour-receiving cones in our retinas are concentrated in the centre of our eyes, our night vision works best when we do not

Opposite page More often than not, lions baffle their human observers with their choice of direction when they set out to hunt – usually diametrically opposite to concentrations of prey.

Above *A full moon usually means inactivity for the lions, as they prefer to hunt during dark nights.*

Opposite above *The lions occasionally show interest in porcupines but then make little attempt to touch them.*

Opposite below *As the sun goes down and the air cools the lions begin to rise and stretch their muscles. Sometimes their nocturnal wanderings will take them five kilometres or more, at other times they may move less than a kilometre away.*

look directly at the object. Lions have far fewer cones in their retinas, but the increased numbers of light-receiving rods give them a distinct advantage at night. Added to this is the tapetal membrane, which reflects available light back onto the retina. The result is that lions probably have night vision comparable to that of domestic cats, which has been estimated to be six times better than ours. This level of night vision is astounding, and even a night with a half moon is probably comparable to a day with some cloud cover in terms of human vision. Add to this highly developed senses of smell and hearing, and one is dealing with a formidable predator.

Lions in general are more successful when they hunt at night than during the day, and also have higher success rates when they hunt in areas where there is good cover like bushes and thickets. The Serengeti studies have also shown that lions have a differential success rate when hunting their main prey species: alert and fast animals like topi

(tsessebe) are caught with the least success per hunting attempt, while warthog, wildebeest and zebra are caught more frequently. This is similar to our observations in the Okavango: tsessebe most frequently escape hunting lions, while warthogs are most frequently caught. These kinds of data are difficult to compile, however, since it is not easy for a human observer to determine what constitutes a serious hunt. Lions encountering a herd of zebra might begin to stalk them, but then lie down and allow them to walk away. Similarly, a group of lions might walk up to a buffalo herd, watch them for a while, and then leave again. Lions have on occasion shown great interest in porcupines, but then made little attempt to touch them. Also, single lions in a group might begin a stalk, but then give up when others in the pride show no interest in participating.

At the other extreme, a group of resting lions are sometimes surprised by a warthog or impala that blunders into their midst and is grabbed almost reflexively. Finally, lions carefully stalking a herd of

impala might fortuitously catch a warthog – is this a successful warthog hunt or a failed impala hunt? There is little doubt, however, that lions make conscious decisions to evaluate their chances of success with various prey species. Ostriches are good examples: to date, the Santawani pride has managed to kill two ostriches, but these swift and nimble birds are very rarely stalked. Tsessebe are often stalked, but the hunt is usually abandoned without an attempt to chase these prey. Warthog, baboon and impala usually elicit a more determined pursuit, as lions seem to have learned that the race is not run in the first few feet.

Why do lions hunt primarily at night? As mentioned, while lions have excellent night vision, their prey are probably able to match them in this regard. Despite their acuity, however, low light levels probably benefit the predators more than their prey. A concealed, motionless or stalking predator must be much more difficult to see on a dark night, and lions can probably run longer distances in the

cool of the night than in the heat of the day. When lions rely on confusion and panic to trap their prey, this is also likely to be achieved more easily at night than during the day. Lions have similar advantages when the normally acute smell and hearing of their prey are compromised during rainstorms, for example.

Above Although the African lion is not yet endangered, it has lost more of its ancestral range than any other terrestrial mammal.

Right Sometimes animals blunder into a whole pride of resting lions. A passing tsessebe initiates an immediate response.

In the dry season, another factor might come into play to render prey more vulnerable. Lions maintain their body temperature by panting, requiring the use of moisture which they replenish with the body fluids of their prey. Antelope have little ability to replace lost moisture in the dry season, and many species have evolved the ability to store heat during the day, and then allow themselves to gradually cool off at night. After a hot day, therefore, antelopes are probably at a considerable disadvantage in terms of their ability to run fast and long from lions. We would expect therefore, all things being equal, that antelope would be killed earlier in the night during the hot summer months than in the winter.

In addition to their vision, lions use also use their sense of hearing when hunting, and we are constantly amazed at how keen this sense is. One day, a pack of wild dogs killed an impala in our camp, without making any discernibly (to the human observers) loud noise. Chris was with a group of subadult lions resting two kilometres away who suddenly pricked up their ears and headed towards the kill at a trot. Unerringly, they found and appropriated the impala within five minutes of the

wild dogs killing it. On other occasions, some members of the pride have made kills and been joined shortly after by other pride members not within the range of reception of their radiocollars (usually two to three kilometres). No other cues but the sounds of the lions feeding would have been available to the late arrivals, who again unerringly found their way to the carcass. When we undertake lion population counts in the Okavango area, the amplified playbacks of recorded hyena sounds on a kill or buffalo distress calls attract lions from distances up to four kilometres away. Their sense of direction in approaching these sounds is uncanny: we play the sounds for 15 minutes followed by 10 minutes of silence, yet the lions are able to find their way directly to the bait even when they are not guided by the playbacks.

Vision also plays an important role in another means by which lions acquire their food - scavenging. Scavenging is usually considered an easy way to get a meal, since the animal has already died of natural causes or been killed by another predator. The inherent risks of injury while hunting are thus avoided. On the open plains of the Serengeti, the

Right King raptor: the lappet-faced vulture is the largest of the raptors and usually dominates over other vultures at carcasses.

Below Mistakenly despised for their scavenging and cowardly nature, hyenas are considered a symbol of death on the African plains.

Masai Mara, and the floor of the Ngorongoro Crater, lions scavenge a high percentage of their meals from hyenas, wild dogs and cheetahs. In many instances, lions are able to witness the hunt itself and chase the other predators off the carcass once the prey has been killed. In more densely vegetated habitats like the Okavango, lions rely on the behaviour of vultures to locate carcasses or kills made by other species. Lions are amazingly alert to flying vultures, even when they are mere specks in the sky. Descending vultures are immediately followed, even over distances of two to three kilometres. The urge to follow descending vultures can at times be overpowering: once we saw a female lion leave a wildebeest kill she was sharing with her pride to follow vultures descending on a juvenile reedbuck kill made by a cheetah half a kilometre away.

Other predators

Because of their size and the likely presence of pride mates, lions have no serious competitor excepting man. Nevertheless, lions act aggressively towards other predators, and will kill adults and young of cheetahs, leopards, wild dogs and hyenas. In the Okavango study area, lions are the major source of mortality for wild dogs, who are often attacked by lions when they are hunting or on kills. Similarly, we have recorded five mortalities among hyenas caused by the Santawani pride alone: all the hyenas were killed when they ventured too close to feeding lions, or in one case, when the hyena walked into a resting group of lions lying a few hundred metres away from a giraffe carcass. The large predators generally avoid each other: wild dogs hunt mostly in the morning and late after-

Below Running battles between lions and hyenas are not common in the Okavango. Only rarely are hyenas present at lion kills, and are always cowed by the lions.

noon; cheetahs usually also hunt during the day but are more active than wild dogs in the middle of the day; leopards and hyenas generally hunt at night, as do lions not in proximity to water.

In the mosaic of habitats of the Okavango, there is perhaps less habitat separation among predators than in other locations where carnivores have been studied, and as a result, the rate at which different predators encounter each other is probably higher. Nevertheless, leopards frequent forests and thickets much more than lions do, and cheetahs are more likely to be found on open plains with little cover where a lion would have difficulty hunting. The large predators also have quite different hunting methods. Leopards, like lions, are adapted to capture prey by using cover to make a close approach, and then use their strength to overpower the animal after a short rush. Cheetahs also stalk their prey, but their comparatively long and slender legs and bodies combined with a highly flexible spine allow them to undertake much longer chases at high speed. Wild dogs are coursers that rely mostly on speed and stamina to chase down their prey, and make little attempt to use cover when hunting. Hyenas hunt in a similar fashion, although they are not able to achieve the running speed of wild dogs.

Hyenas are the most interactive of all the large predator species, and turn up at a considerable percentage of all cheetah, wild dog and lion kills. Their aim is, of course, to scavenge as much as possible from these kills, and wherever possible to drive off the original predators and appropriate their prey. Much has been made of the 'animosity' existing between lions and hyenas based on frequent encounters between these two species in Savuti, an area to the northeast of the Okavango.

Here, daily battles have been recorded, and when the ratio of hyenas to lions exceeded 4:1, the hyenas were frequently able to drive lions off their kills, sometimes even inflicting wounds and casualties. In the Okavango study area, we have never seen hyenas chase lions from their kills, even when the hyenas greatly outnumbered the feeding lions.

A few examples can be given to illustrate this point. An elephant had died close to the border of the Moremi Game Reserve in October 1995. Two female lions and a young cub from the Mogogelo

pride had discovered the carcass, and fed on it through the early evening. As night began to settle, a large number of hyenas gathered, until there were 27 present at the carcass.

The hyenas made several attempts to chase the lions off, but scampered away every time the lionesses made a charge at them. This went on for about two hours, before the hyenas began to leave of their own accord. The next morning the lions were still at the carcass, and only two hyenas remained, lying some distance away.

Above Confrontations between lions and hyenas at kills invariably end with the hyenas backing off.
Opposite far left In the tree the leopard's meal is safe from marauding hyenas and lions.
Opposite middle The cheetah also stalks its prey, but the final burst of speed is electrifying.

Below *Hyena society is dominated by the females and the matriarch's female cub will automatically succeed her, when fully grown.*

Below right *Hyenas are more closely related to the mongoose family than to cats or dogs. Their social system is much more orderly than that of lions.*

Opposite *The Santawani airstrip clan descend on a wildebeest, eating it alive. Hyenas are ruthless hunters and run their prey down through sheer perseverance.*

On another occasion, three adult lionesses and five subadults of the Santawani pride had killed a tsessebe close to camp. The lions ate their fill and most moved off to lie some 30 metres away. Two 20-month old males remained eating the skin, closely watched by 22 hyenas. Every time the hyenas attempted to take over the remains of the carcass, they were repulsed by the young males, until they finally ambled away. Hyenas are generally the first to arrive when we use calling stations to estimate lion numbers in the Okavango area. On no occasion have these hyenas been able to keep lions off the bait, even on occasions when they outnumbered the lions 10 or 15 to one. This is not to say that large numbers of hyenas are not on occasion able to take kills from a single lion or a small group. Such interactions have been observed in the Okavango area as well as other study sites like the Serengeti. Our point is that such occasions are far from the norm.

Why then, did this happen with such regularity in Savuti? We believe these observations were made under an unusual set of circumstances. Savuti used to contain an extensive marsh, fed by the Savuti Channel. Water flow into the Savuti marsh was interrupted, possibly as a result of lower overall water levels, a blockage upstream, tectonic shifts, or a combination of these factors. The Savuti marsh began to dry up, and as a result, an area that had seen very high densities of prey animals now became much more seasonal in terms of presence of ungulates. Most of the large resident prey animals like buffalo, wildebeest and zebra moved out of the area, leaving behind a relatively dense large predator population that had been established when conditions were good. Predators, being territorial, did not have recourse to migration to better areas to the north and west. As a result, a situation was created whereby a high-density predator population existed in an area with seasonally very low prey densities. No better conditions could be created to increase levels of competition between lions and hyenas, as any kill or carcass was now a scarce resource. Interactions between lions and hyenas could therefore have been predicted to escalate, and a combination of hunger and experience probably

made hyenas much more bold around lions than in other areas. Suffice it to say that while this situation might have received considerable publicity, it is certainly not representative of the usual level or course of interaction between these carnivores.

Hunting is not an easy way to make a living. Lions, despite their size, strength, and long apprenticeship, have lower hunting success than other predators like wild dogs. Prey animals are canny, careful and quick. Because of their body size, lions can hunt a diversity of prey species, but each presents unique challenges.

Lions try to maximise their success by hunting vulnerable prey or those that place themselves in a position of danger by their need to drink. Also because of their body size, they have no serious competitors and can usually pilfer prey from other predators; because of their visual acuity, they often use distant vultures to guide them to carcasses. They can hunt by day or night, depending on environmental conditions, and even neighbouring prides may be radically different in the kinds of prey animals they catch. Only man presents a threat to their future.

Following pages There is a misconception that predators like lions only remove the old, sick or weak members of prey populations. Predators are opportunists and will take advantage of any chance they get, in this case a rare roan antelope.

The future

As mentioned in the Introduction, conservation of lions is a pressing issue. In the future, Africa's lion populations can only decline: close to 100 lions are shot as problem animals each year in Botswana alone, and the situation in other range states is not likely to be different. Few African countries have the capability to reduce the pressure of rural people on land by offering alternative living and earning opportunities in cities. Damaging agricultural schemes and overgrazing by livestock will put escalating pressure on land now set aside for wildlife.

African governments are increasingly having to tread a fine line between the demands of their citizens for land and their own conservation priorities, determined to a large extent by income from tourism. Encroachment of cattle on reserves like the Masai Mara and Amboseli in Kenya is now the norm, and the erection of fences around reserves is an increasingly common solution to wildlife-livestock conflicts. The consequences of further and further reducing the areas available to predator species will be considerable, and given our current lack of knowledge about the workings of even simple ecological systems, potentially disastrous.

Nothing said above is particularly new: with the exception of the recovery of East African elephant populations following the removal of economic incentives for poaching, there are few success stories in African wildlife conservation. Conservation-minded bodies have made considerable strides on political fronts, but the much-vaunted Convention on Biodiversity has achieved little. Though a plethora of schemes are now in existence to involve rural communities in the maintenance of wildlife resources, the biosphere concept (considering humans and wildlife as ecological partners) is bound to fail in the case of dangerous predators. Moreover, these programmes have not proceeded hand-in-hand with acquisition of much-needed information on the animals themselves, which is dangerously shortsighted.

Above Shades of evening turn the trees a deeper brown. As night falls, the woods echo to the roar of the lion.

Opposite The skull of Shiraz. Since his death new males have established themselves with his former prides on the Gomoti and Mogogelo.

Disease control

One example of our lack of information concerns the increasing danger domestic animal diseases pose to wildlife. The concept of diseases flowing from domestic animal reservoirs to wild animals is relatively new: in Africa, wildlife was always blamed for outbreaks of foot-and-mouth disease, African horse sickness, African swine fever and theileriosis among domestic stock. Attempts to control diseases threatening livestock often involved draconian measures. For example, over 60 000 wild ungulates were shot around Maun in Botswana between 1942 and 1964 in an ultimately completely unsuccessful attempt to control tsetse flies. While it is true that wildlife populations can harbour a diversity of diseases, one of the greatest disasters ever to befall wildlife and livestock was caused by a massive outbreak of rinderpest at the turn of the century: the disease did not originate with wildlife, but was introduced by cattle. Similarly, there is now clear genetic evidence that the most common African rabies virus strain was established by importation of infected dogs from Europe.

In these days of spatially confined wildlife populations, transmission of diseases from domestic animal populations can have devastating consequences. An outbreak of a genetically variant canine distemper virus capable of infecting felids caused the death of an estimated 1 000 lions in the Serengeti in 1994: the source of this virus was believed to be domestic dogs living around the reserve. The virus has since caused mortality among lions in the Masai Mara, and is likely to continue its spread through susceptible lion populations in other parts of Tanzania and Kenya. Despite the recorded incidence of canine distemper among domestic dogs in Kenya and Tanzania, the potential of this virus to cause mortality among felids caught everyone flat-footed. As an example of the danger cattle populations can pose to wildlife, a recent outbreak of bovine pleuropneumonia in Botswana was only controlled by a massive effort involving the erection of containment fences and destruction of an estimated 300 000 head of cattle. If this outbreak had involved a disease capable of infecting wildlife, the outcome would have been disastrous.

Right *A young lion displays a perfect set of teeth. As lions get older they will often lose incisors, and canines frequently break or become blunted. Abcessed teeth are common among older lions.*

Opposite *The texture of a lion's tongue is very abrasive. After the tensions at a kill, communal cleaning and grooming restore the harmony within the pride.*

Above *A fine grey dust envelops the scene as a hyena chases vultures off a carcass. This carnivore is the lion's main competitor.*

Right *The whole Delta ecosystem is entirely dependent on the Okavango's floodwater. Without it there will be no herds of big game for the lions to hunt.*

Documenting the incidence of disease among wild animals is extremely difficult. Carcasses necessary for diagnosis are rapidly destroyed by scavengers like hyenas and vultures, and the usual method of recording diseases is to conduct antibody surveys. Antibodies are formed by the immune system in response to challenges by a pathogen, and can be detected by taking blood samples from target animals. Presence of antibodies usually means the sampled animal's immune system has successfully dealt with the infection, but by monitoring antibody levels in known individuals over time, one can gain important information about the ecology of the disease in question.

For example, if antibody concentrations fall off over time, the disease was probably present only temporarily, whereas uniform or increasing concentrations can be taken to indicate a more constant presence of the pathogen. Sampling wild animals involves considerable effort and cost, and is by nature invasive. Nevertheless, such studies are of increasing importance and are becoming crucial to informed wildlife management.

Lions sampled in Botswana indicate there has been a high level of exposure to feline herpes virus (96 per cent of 53 individuals sampled were antibody-positive), feline immunodeficiency virus (42 per cent) and canine distemper virus (26 per cent). These samples were all taken from apparently healthy individuals, and the potential effects and origins of infection with these pathogens is as yet

uncertain. Studies on captive felids have shown that large cats infected with feline herpes virus and feline immunodeficiency virus can suffer negative consequences. The incidence of canine distemper virus antibodies among free-ranging lions in Botswana is both interesting and worrisome. No mortality has to date resulted, and it is likely that the virus is not of the same type that infected lions in Tanzania. However, it clearly indicates that, as in Tanzania, lions in Botswana do come in contact with domestic dog diseases. Retrospective surveys indicated that lions in the Serengeti had come into contact with canine distemper long before the outbreak involving the new viral strain. We think it likely that the virus is passed to lions through intermediary hosts like jackals: these small canids

Above *Canine distemper virus can be passed through intermediary hosts like jackals. These small canids can pick up the disease when they scavenge around villages and then pass it on to lions when they come into contact at kills.*

Right *These young pups have no worries. Being supreme opportunists, jackals still roam across the whole of Africa.*

Opposite above *All social carnivores are particularly vulnerable to disease. Whole populations of wild dogs have been wiped out in Kenya and Botswana during the last decade.*

Opposite below *Imitating its parents, a pup howls out the eerie jackal cry that is often heard at dusk.*

could pick up the disease when they scavenge around villages, and then pass it to lions when they come into contact at kills. If the Tanzanian virus is ever introduced into Botswana, an established conduit thus exists to facilitate transfer of the disease from domestic dogs living around reserves to lion populations inside these reserves.

Diseases can be controlled by vaccination, but the prospect of mounting an effective campaign in this instance is minimal. Domestic dogs are not an economic resource like cattle, and it is unlikely that the manpower and funds would be mobilised and maintained to ensure effective vaccination of the large domestic dog population around the Okavango. Discontinuing such a vaccination campaign at any point is more dangerous than not

starting one at all, as this could create an even larger population of susceptible animals. Vaccinating the lions themselves is if anything more difficult: canine distemper vaccine must be administered annually, and requires the ability to accurately recognise individual lions. Also, the dosage required, potential side effects, and whether the lion's immune system will make sufficient levels of antibodies to be protective in the event of a natural outbreak are all unknown. Distemper spreads best under conditions of high host densities, and where the movement of infected animals allows infection of new populations. Just as controls on the movement of livestock have proved a simple and effective means of curbing the spread of diseases, outbreaks of distemper could be minimised by strict controls on the movement of domestic dogs into wildlife management areas.

Diseases also cause problems with translocations and reintroductions. So many Kruger lions now test positive for antibodies to feline immunodeficiency virus that there is a strong reluctance to use individuals from this lion population to restock other areas. As mentioned, almost half of the Botswana lions are also antibody-positive. Only Etosha National Park lions thus far show no evidence of having been infected, but so little is yet known about the genetic structure of southern African lion populations that it would be ill-advised to introduce Namibian animals wherever space for lions is available.

Maintenance of biodiversity

The maintenance of biodiversity includes the maintenance of established genetic diversity, and only in extreme circumstances is it justified to mix individuals from geographically separated populations. George Adamson's work with lions in Kenya might have been popular with the layman, but was a complete genetic tragedy in that lions

Above Solid shade is hard to find in the sweltering heat of October. This baobab tree is a favourite resting place for the lions of the Mogogelo.

Opposite Cloud and a cool breeze bring welcome relief. Another year passes and the rainy season begins again.

with a southern African genetic makeup were introduced into Kenya. Some of the introduced lions bred with residents, and the Born Free legacy now includes a population of mixed eastern and southern African genotypes living in the area. This is an unnatural genetic combination, but the mistake was made before the studies were done to show that eastern and southern African lion populations are genetically different from each other. The same mistake has been made since then, however, and ignorance is no excuse. Lions are now being bred for 'sport' hunting, but these programmes should be carefully monitored to prevent mixing of distinct genotypes. We are not strict adaptationists who believe that every difference has an adaptive value, but we do believe that we should not tinker with what we do not yet understand.

Lions emigrating from their natal areas are essential in the maintenance of gene flow between populations. As populations become more confined such dispersers often find themselves unwelcome trespassers in agricultural or livestock areas. Small reserves in particular will have problems maintaining a sufficient number of lions to prevent inbreeding, and some South African reserves have had to resort to sterilisation of males to prevent them breeding with daughters and granddaughters. Females in these reserves would then be artificially inseminated with sperm collected from males in other locations. Young males and females born in these small reserves cannot emigrate and cannot be introduced into other reserves that already have lions: such introductions would involve consider-

Left *Baronne was four years old when he was finally persuaded to leave his natal pride. Within one year he was dead.*

Opposite left *The lions frequently visited camp after dark and, while they would be docile during the day, their personalities changed completely at night.*

Opposite right *Excessive pressure from tourists can be highly disruptive to lions' lives. Despite all appearances lions are vulnerable to a variety of stresses.*

able risks of injuries and mortalities among both introduced and resident lions. Lion populations in small reserves can thus only exist as rather artificial groups, requiring invasive techniques to maintain any kind of genetic integrity. Only lions in large reserves will do well in the future.

In many southern and eastern African countries, lions continue to be hunted as trophy animals. As stated, lions are difficult animals to hunt sustainably, as the consequence of shooting a pride male can involve subsequent death of cubs when other males take over from the weakened coalition. In addition, reproductive success of females can be compromised for some time after new males take over a pride. The consequences of excessively high hunting quotas are already being noticed in Tanzania, where younger and younger male lions are being shot. The Botswana government, however, has now combined a policy of low quotas with regular lion population surveys, which will ultimately contribute greatly to a level of lion hunting which is sustainable. Carefully managed trophy hunting will not threaten lion populations in the Okavango, but continued monitoring of hunted populations is essential.

More worrisome in both the long and short term is the large number of lions shot each year as problem animals. Botswana compensates farmers for

Right Fallen trees are often used as vantage points and supply an opportunity to sharpen claws.

Below The soft pads under a lion's paw measure about 12 cm on average. Although rough in texture, they are sensitive.

livestock lost to predators like hyenas and lions, but also allows the farmers to shoot predators. In addition, the Department of Wildlife and National Parks often sends out teams of its own hunters in response to complaints from farmers.

In Namibia, research done on stock-raiding lions concluded that these animals can be divided into two categories: occasional and habitual problem animals. In the case of occasional problem animals, many of which had taken a foray into livestock areas from their usual haunts in reserves, strong measures taken to harass and scare off the lions were sufficient to dissuade them from future livestock raids. Habitual stock raiders, however, had to be destroyed, as no amount of coercion could deter them. Such measures should be instituted in Botswana: the current double indemnity system of providing compensation and shooting lions must be discontinued. If compensation is to be provided, dissuasion of stock-raiding lions should be attempted before destroying them.

Preserving wilderness

With so much already lost, the emphasis should be on maintaining truly wild populations. This will require a much more intimate knowledge of individual species and the workings of ecosystems than we have today. Good conservation policies also need to include an evaluation of the diseases circulating among domestic animal populations around reserves, as even the best management plans for animals in reserves can be compromised by a single epidemic.

All predators should be treated as endangered species: they should not have to wait to 'deserve' the status when populations have dropped to alarmingly low levels. It is not difficult to comprehend that there are better conservation prospects for a species that still has some healthy populations left than for those that need ultimately costly emergency measures to keep a few remaining individuals alive. If trophy hunting is carefully monitored, the additional land available to lions in the form of hunting concessions can be considered a benefit.

Above Lions of the South Pan pride drink from the shrinking water of a pan in the heart of the Santawani pride's territory.

Despite all appearances, lions are fragile animals vulnerable to a variety of stresses, and this is a point to be considered by the photographic tourism industry in particular. We have all by now heard the dictum 'shoot me once but photograph me a thousand times': in some heavy-usage tourist areas, the lions themselves might amend that to 'please shoot me now rather than letting me die a thousand deaths'. There are few sights as depressing as a group of lions trying to ignore a circle of tourist vehicles during the day, and then being additionally harassed at night with spotlights. All sectors of the wildlife industry have an obligation to best protect the goose that is providing them with golden eggs, and this includes the hunting and photographic sectors as well as the local communities.

The toolkit we carry around with us when we engage in a study of lions has many drawers, each of which will be opened during our future work. The genetic drawer has the probes and markers to be able to accurately determine cub paternity and maternity, relationships among males in a coalition and females in a pride, and levels of genetic diversity and resemblance among populations of lions in Botswana. The disease drawer has the kits to determine the prevalence and levels of a variety of antibodies, and is opened to monitor domestic dogs as well as jackals, leopards and lions. The reproductive drawer contains the assays to determine reproductive and stress hormone levels, and there are also drawers with tools to study ecology and behaviour. The toolkit is expandable, and has room for drawers on physiology, immunology and parasitology.

We cannot do all this alone, and rely on a network of collaborators who are leaders in their fields. This will ensure that our suggestions on how best to conserve lions will be comprehensive and relevant. Effective conservation will only result if governments and wildlife users have a genuine interest in implementing suggestions. Botswana probably has the largest lion population left in southern Africa, and therefore the population that is most likely to survive well into the future. This is both a blessing and a liability, and places a heavy responsibility on the government and citizens of Botswana, together with researchers, conservation organisations, safari operators and hunters. The continued presence of lions in Botswana is to a large extent dependent on how well we cooperate to ensure their future.

Left *Lions frequently use man-made tracks, but what does the future hold for lions further down the road?*

Bibliography

Bertram, B C, 1975. 'Social factors influencing reproduction in wild lions', *Journal of Zoology*, London, 177: 463-82.

Bygott, J D, B C Bertram and J P Hanby, 1979. 'Male lions in large coalitions gain reproductive advantages', *Nature* 282: 839-41.

Child, G, P Smith and W von Richter, 'Tsetse control hunting as a measure of large mammal population trends in the Okavango Delta, Botswana', *Mammalia* 34: 34-74.

Cooper, S M, 1991. 'Optimal hunting group size: the need for lions to defend their kills against loss to spotted hyenas', *African Journal of Ecology* 29: 130-6.

Dawkins, R, 1982. *The Extended Phenotype.* Oxford: Oxford University Press.

Gilbert, D A, C Packer, A E Pusey, J C Stephens and S J O'Brien, 1991. 'Analytical DNA fingerprinting in lions: parentage, genetic diversity, and kinship', *Journal of Heredity* 82: 378-86.

Grinnell, J and K McComb, 1996. 'Maternal grouping as a defense against infanticide by males: evidence from field playback experiments on African lions', *Behavioral Ecology* 7: 55-9.

Hanby, J P and J D Bygott, 1987. 'Emigration of subadult lions', *Animal Behavior* 35: 161-9.

Natoli, E, 1990. 'Mating strategies in cats: a comparison of the role and importance of infanticide in domestic cats, *Felis catus L*, and lions, *Panthera leo L*', *Animal Behavior* 40: 183-5.

Packer, C and A E Pusey, 1982. 'Cooperation and competition within coalitions of male lions: kin selection or game theory?' *Nature* 296: 740-2.

– 1983. 'Adaptations of female lions to infanticide by incoming males', *The American Naturalist* 121: 716-28.

– 1993. 'Dispersal, kinship, and inbreeding in African lions', pp 375-91 in *Inbreeding and Outbreeding: Theoretical and Empirical Perspectives.* Chicago: University of Chicago Press.

Packer, C, D Scheel and A E Pusey, 1990. 'Why lions form groups: food is not enough', *The American Naturalist* 136: 1-19.

Packer, C, D A Gilbert, A E Pusey and S J O'Brien, 1991. 'A molecular genetic analysis of kinship and cooperation in African lions', *Nature* 351: 562-5.

Pusey, A E and C Packer, 1987. 'The evolution of sex-biased dispersal in lions', *Behaviour* 101: 275-307.

Schaller, G B, 1972. *The Serengeti Lion.* Chicago: University of Chicago Press.

Scheel, D and C Packer, 1991. 'Group hunting behaviour of lions: a search for cooperation', *Animal Behavior* 41: 697-709.

Schmidt, A M, D L Hess, M J Schmidt, R C Smith and C R Lewis, 1988. 'Serum concentrations of oestradiol and progesterone, and sexual behaviour during the normal oestrus cycle in the leopard (*Panthera pardus*)', *Journal of Reproduction and Fertility* 82: 43-9.

Schmidt, P M, P K Chakraborty and D E Wildt, 1983. 'Ovarian activity, circulating hormones, and sexual behavior in the cat. II. Relationships during pregnancy, parturition, lactation, and the postpartum estrus', *Biology of Reproduction* 28: 657-71.

Schramm, R D, M B Briggs and J J Reeves, 1994. 'Spontaneous and induced ovulation in the lion (*Panthera leo*)', *Zoo Biology* 13: 301-7.

Stander, P, 1990. 'A suggested management strategy for stock-raiding lions in Namibia', *South African Journal of Wildlife Research* 20: 37-43.

– 1992. 'Foraging dynamics of lions in a semi-arid environment', *Canadian Journal of Zoology* 70: 8-21.

Wildt, D E, S W J Seager and P K Chakraborty, 1980. 'Effect of copulatory stimuli on incidence of ovulation and on serum luteinizing hormone in the cat', *Endocrinology* 107: 1212-16.

Yamazaki, K, 1996. 'Social variation of lions in a male-depopulated area in Zambia', *Journal of Wildlife Management* 60: 490-7.

Acknowledgements

First and foremost, I would like to thank the Government of Botswana for the opportunity to live and conduct research in that country. The Office of the President and Lieutenant General S.K.I. Khama, Vice President and Minister for Presidential Affairs and Public Administration have been especially supportive through the years. The endorsement of this project by the Botswana Department of Wildlife and National Parks has smoothed many obstacles. Within the DWNP, I would especially like to thank Sedia Modise, Joe Mathlare, Rapelang Mojaphoko, Abraham Modho, Dan Mughogho, and Lucas Rutina.

Nicole Apelian worked hard and long as a volunteer during the early days of the project for little more than her love of the lions. Also, many Maun residents have helped the project in a diversity of ways. I would especially like to thank Tim and Bryony Longden, Dougie and Diane Wright, Chris Collins, Hennie Visser, Mark and Mary-Lou Kyriacou, Allison van Niekerk, Karl-Heinz Gimpel, Lionel Palmer, Harry Selby, the late Neville Peake, Debbie Peake, Karen Ross, Jens Kuhn, Johan Knols, and Annelies Zonjee. Tico McNutt helped tremendously in getting the project started, and Gametrackers Botswana provided accommodation at Santawani lodge during the early days of the project. Crocodile Camp Safaris and the Sankuyu Community have since allowed us to establish camp within their concession area.

Securing funding for projects like these is always difficult in the beginning stages, but we have been fortunate in always managing to patch things together and keep going. Our gratitude is especially extended to the Philadelphia Zoo, Rodney Fuhr, the Denver Zoo, the Okavango Wild Life Society, Ken Musgrave and the Seebe Trust, Steve Goodman, John Laing and the Rufford Foundation, and Keith Leggett and the Kalahari Conservation Society.

Kate Nicholls, Travers McNeice, Angus McNeice, Maisie McNeice, and Oakley Purchase are my family in the bush, and without their support, care, and love, none of this would have been possible. Kate combines many unique talents, not the least of which are a comprehensive understanding of lion reproduction, how to live well in our home in the bush, how to keep things going on a shoestring, and how to revive flagging spirits when the lions are unfindable, the camp is sodden after days of rain, and the bank is rejecting yet another loan application. Kate is the 'we' in the text and her perceptiveness about the lions has led to many new research directions. I am only fortunate to have found a partner like her.

PIETER KAT

I am extremely grateful to the Office of the President of Botswana and to the Department of Wildlife and National Parks for allowing me to photograph in the Moremi Game Reserve, in particular J. Sethibe and Sedia Modise.

I especially would like to thank Ronnie Crous of Crocodile Camp Safaris for allowing me to photograph in their concession area. Tim Read, Margi Barnardt of Gametrackers Botswana for allowing us to use the lodge at Santawani and the staff there: Witness Masasa, Sam Samoxa, Josekwang Dilao, Prescilla Boitume and to Dougie and Diane Wright of Ker and Downey Botswana for their many years of help.

At Southern Book Publishers my appreciation goes to Louise Grantham for her faith in this project and to Reneé Ferreira and Lyndall du Toit for their patience and hard work in putting the book together.

Also I wish to thank Peter Perlstein of Wildlife Helicopters. His renowned flying skill contributed greatly to the aerial photography. Also to John and Tina Davey, John and Elaine Dugmore, Chris Collins, Tico and Lesley McNutt, Karen Ross, Julian Cooke, Lionel Palmer, Ken and Mel Oake, Steve Empsom, Mathew Hutchings, Ron Keys, David Keys, Bernard and Paula Price, John Baxter, James Bisset, Mike and Fran Slabber, Alistair and Dawn Sholto-Douglas, Roger and Jacquie Moston, Dorothy Fluke, Graham Williams, Berni Vendt and Rob Farrar at Alchemy Studios, and my family – Doreen, Verna, Ben.

Finally to my wife Maggi for her support during all the years of frustrations, hardships and elations that are part of life in the bush... and, of course, the lions.

CHRIS HARVEY

Photographer's Notes

If I have learnt anything it is that the greatest memory lies in the moment of observation, and that experience can never be reproduced in a picture.

I have been privileged to have been able to record the private lives of lions in a pristine wilderness, where few vehicles have ever been. Initially this proved to be a handicap as the lions were shy and retiring. Eventually we gained their trust and the photography became easier, however, we pledged to respect their needs in return for their tolerance. Lions depend on their acute senses to survive. To their ears a vehicle is noisy and confuses informa-

tion that their hearing is tuned to. Thoughtless parking in front of them may obstruct their vision over an open plain and at night a rumbling exhaust and bright lights can alert potential prey as well as disturbing the lions' night vision. Cats' eyes are six times more sensitive to light than humans'. Lights can also 'blind' their prey, making it an unnatural kill. It is known that lions can become dependent on lights at night when they are regularly followed. Occasionally lions may find a vehicle a temporary source of interest but, most of the time, they would definitely prefer to be without us, no matter how much we kid ourselves that we have been accepted as 'friends' or 'part of the pride'. These are purely human fantasies and the reality is that lions have no need of us at all and by imagining that we have, in some way, tamed them is to corrupt the very freedom and wildness that we have come to photograph.

A native American Indian chief, commenting on the loss of his people's ancient hunting grounds to European settlers in the 19th century, told of how his people used to live in harmony with the wilderness and that the west only became 'wild' after the white man had tamed it.

So what price to get a picture? I have tried to record the behaviour of these lions as an observer during this time and was always concerned not to unduly harass them. There is no doubt that any human contact with wild animals is going to affect the naturalness and there is a strong case for restricting the amount of traffic in wildlife reserves. It is also clear that lions need places within reserves where they will not be disturbed by people and so can be left 'untamed'.

For the record: All photographs were taken with Canon EOS 1 and 5 cameras with f2.8 300mm lens, 2x and 1.4x converters, and 80-210mm and 20-35mm zoom lenses by Canon. Flash equipment was manufactured by Norman USA and film used was Kodak Ektachrome 100SW.

Index